PRAISE FROM THE MED
FOR JAN

"Jan King's unique and inventive brand of humor will uplift the reader."
—Philomena McAndrew, M.D.

"Jan King is a survivor who takes life with double strides. Her recovery after breast cancer has been inspirational and exemplifies her pathway toward positive physical and mental well-being. It's been my experience that patients with this 'go-forth attitude' return to mainstream life quickly and most importantly—survive. Thanks, Jan, for sharing your philosophy."
—Thomas P. Sokol, M.D.

"Cancer is a devastating illness, both physically and mentally. Jan King is living proof that not only can cancer be defeated with exercise, diet and a positive mental state, but the entire recovery process can be improved and expedited."
—Herbert I. Stein, M.D.

"Ms. King is a perfect example of the uncommon individual who has achieved balance in her life. A more exuberant, optimistic, and positive person would be hard to find. Her zest for life is contagious!.
—Joseph Lebovic, M.D.

"Jan's indefatigable stamina and incredibly positive attitude are strong allies in the fight against any disease or any of life's obstacles. She never misses a beat, and if the power of her energy could be bottled as a medicine to others, it most certainly would be given universally."
—Sharon A. Winer, M.D., M.P.H.

To Richard —
So happy to meet you at AB —
stay well & happy —
Best [signature]

BOUNCING BACK

Rebound from
Life's Challenges
with Humor,
Grace, and Style

To Dr Thomas —
Hope you enjoy!
Best, [signature]

OTHER BOOKS BY JAN KING:

Hormones From Hell

It's A Girl Thing

When You're Hot, You're Hot

It's A Mom Thing

Red Hot Mamas

BOUNCING BACK

*Rebound from
Life's Challenges
with Humor,
Grace, and Style*

by Jan King

RUNNING PRESS
PHILADELPHIA · LONDON

9   8   7   6   5   4   3   2   1
Digit on the right indicates the number of this printing

Library of Congress Control Number: 2005937033

ISBN-13: 978-0-7624-2614-0
ISBN-10: 0-7624-2614-4

Book Design by Amanda Richmond
Edited by Jennifer Kasius
Cover photograph by Charles William Bush
Hairstylist: Carolyn Caroll
Makeup: 'Jus Judy

This book may be ordered by mail from the publisher.
Please include $2.50 for postage and handling.
But try your bookstore first!

Running Press Book Publishers
125 South Twenty-Second Street
Philadelphia, Pennsylvania 19103-4399

Visit us on the web!
www.runningpress.com

TABLE *of* CONTENTS

Acknowledgments . . .11

Introduction . . .13

Presenting: The Bounce Plan of Action . . .17

PART I: *The Issues*

Illness: Physical

Chapter 1: Cancer: My Time At Bat . . .29

Chapter 2: Getting A Grip: The Stuff You're Made Of . . .33

Chapter 3: Healing: How I Bounced Back . . .41

Loss: Spiritual

Chapter 4: Death Of A Loved One: Healing the Heart . . .53

Chapter 5: Divorce: Loving the Enemy . . .67

Chapter 6: Empty Nest: Your Chance to Fly . . .77

Conflict: Emotional

Chapter 7: Family Conflict: And Justice for All . . .93

Chapter 8: Relationship Struggles: Friendly Fire . . .107

Chapter 9: Inner Conflict: At War With Yourself . . .119

Chapter 10: Positive Thoughts: Positively Create Reality . . .127

PART II: *The Actions*

Chapter 11: Don't Diet: Be Healthy . . .143

Chapter 12: Juicing: The Power Punch . . .155

Chapter 13: Nutritious Foods: The Good Earth . . .163

Chapter 14: Exercise: The Gift That Keeps On Giving . . .177

References . . .190

My love and gratitude to my wonderful friend Gail Fisher, who has helped me discover and continues to guide me on my spiritual path to wellness. You have been an incredibly powerful positive force in my life.

———∿∿∿———

Also, my love and gratitude to my sister, Karen, who unselfishly and unconditionally gives me her time, her wisdom, and her loving support. I could never have bounced back as well as I did without you.

Acknowledgments

To my editor Jennifer Kasius:
Thank you for your incredibly astute insights and suggestions that helped make this book's message crystal clear and easy to follow. I am so fortunate to be working with a young woman who has such wonderful skills and so much wisdom. You totally amaze me! I sure hope we'll be working on many more books together.

To Jon Anderson:
Thanks for always giving me your advice, support, and encouragement. I have learned so much from you over the years, and owe you a debt of gratitude for helping me to continue to evolve in many directions that all make me a better writer.

Introduction

To the outside world, I lead some kind of charmed life. I have an exciting career as an author, I speak at various forums all over the country, my marriage is happy, I have wonderful children and grandchildren, and I am disgustingly healthy. Hey, you know something? I guess they're right.

But no matter how charmed a person's life may appear, one thing I know is true. We all have our *time at bat.* And like everyone else, I've been dealt my share of misery. So far in my life, I've been through two divorces, moved seven times, was diagnosed with breast cancer, had three major surgeries, and borne the losses of my mother and some wonderful friends. Can I expect some more tough times? Sure. As I always say, "The hardest time in a woman's life is from *birth to death.*"

The good news is that I not only survived it all, but now, my life is better than ever before. However, I don't like being called a "survivor." The fact is that my survival was never in question. Luckily, my particular case of breast cancer was caught at stage one. So, truthfully, there wasn't any real danger of me up and dying on the spot.

However, I did undergo bilateral mastectomies and reconstructive surgery. Not exactly a walk in the park.

The point is that throughout the course of our lives, traumas are inevitable. Nobody leads *that* charmed a life to escape her share. We are all going to be challenged, over and over again, with situations causing us emotional and physical pain. Fortunately, most are not as extreme as life or death scenarios, but if they're not handled wisely, they can do some serious damage. Most people are happy just to *get through* these challenges. I think that's not enough. I believe it's not only possible to bounce back, but to emerge stronger than before with a greater appreciation for life.

During my recovery from breast cancer, I became convinced that physical illness isn't just about the physical body. Disease is rooted in emotional and spiritual planes, too. Nowadays, more and more physicians are beginning to share this belief. After doing a great deal of reading and soul-searching, I came to believe that the only way I was going to heal completely and stay healthy was by working through my emotional and spiritual issues to become emotionally sound and spiritually at peace.

The truth is that we need to start realizing that we are more than just our physical bodies. Our emotional and spiritual components are integral parts of who we are and need to be nourished just like our physical side. All three sides profoundly affect the others at all times, and contribute to our wellness or disease.

That's what this book is all about. *Bouncing Back* will teach you how to channel your energy physically, emotionally, and spiritually in ways that allow you to rise above your problems. I will be discussing the most common experiences in life that are particularly difficult to handle. Using my plan, you'll find you are not only able to cope with your problems, but ultimately, you will also triumph over them.

Presenting:

The Bounce Plan of Action

WHEN LIFE BEATS YOU DOWN...

An upsetting event does a lot more than we realize to interfere with the normal functioning of our bodies. Depression, shock, anger, and other emotions have a negative effect on the nervous, digestive, and other systems in the body. In response to a trauma, the brain releases certain chemicals that set up a kind of chain reaction, and ultimately, the entire body is affected in some way.

Scientists have identified certain chemicals in the brain released during trauma that can depress the normal functioning of the immune system. And when the immune system is suppressed, we become susceptible to certain diseases, such as cancer. A well-known example of this is Kaposi's sarcoma, a cancer that manifests itself in a person with a seriously compromised immune system, such as an HIV patient.

We need to keep this fact in mind when we're faced with a crisis. When one occurs, it's crucial that we support our bodies and be kind to ourselves. Often, the instinctive reaction of a body to crisis is to shut down with inactivity and depression.

DON'T BEAT YOURSELF DOWN MORE

It's not uncommon for people to react to a devastating situation with self-destructive behaviors such as drinking, self-medicating with tranquilizers, smoking too many cigarettes, taking amphetamines for a boost, or using painkillers to numb themselves. A person may take to his bed for long stretches of time, hoping to wake up and find that the problem has magically disappeared. However, all of these actions, which seemingly make us feel better, are the *worst* things we can do for ourselves.

Trust me. You don't need any of these crutches to get you through a tough situation. These "quick fixes" will do nothing but keep you stuck in the situation, temporarily numbed by drugs that don't allow you to think clearly and keep you distracted from the problem. To make matters worse, there is the real possibility of becoming physically and emotionally addicted to these medications. If this should happen, any chance of ever resolving the initial problem will be virtually eliminated.

YOU CAN BOUNCE BACK . . .

When a crisis threatens to immobilize you, that's your cue to get moving! Don't just react—act. You cannot allow yourself to get to the point where depression shuts your body down. There are actions you can take—physically, emotionally, and spiritually—that will give you the confidence and energy you need to bounce back.

. . .WITH THE BOUNCE PLAN

From my own experience of going through the traumas I mentioned earlier, I formulated a plan that has been highly effective for me. I've organized the basic principles into an acronym that's easy to remember:

B-O-U-N-C-E

BE POSITIVE:

The old adage "When life throws you a lemon, make lemonade" is one of the most helpful ones I know. When you are able to see a problem as an opportunity to learn and grow, it becomes a lot easier to conquer. Also, when the knowledge you gain from that experience is applied to future problems, your life will work better than ever.

We can all learn something valuable from people like cancer survivors. Because many of them had to face the frightening possibility of losing their lives, they have developed an incredible appreciation for every day they're here. This kind of event makes you re-arrange your priorities very quickly. Take it from me. Life is much sweeter and much less stressful for people who think this way.

OVERCOME STRESS:

When a stressful event occurs, your mind is the key to interpreting the problem and subsequently, choosing which way to act. Meditation is the most helpful way I know to clear the mind and calm the soul, allowing you to think analytically. And, once you are able to think constructively, your actions will be constructive, not destructive.

UPLIFT YOURSELF:

It's a fact that our attitudes and moods are affected by the company we keep. You will find that your life will work much better if you surround yourself with people who genuinely care for you.

People who are constantly embroiled in personal battles and negative situations are energy vampires. Stay clear of them. They will usurp your time and energy, leaving you depleted.

Just as you should choose pure and nontoxic foods to nourish your body, do the same for your mind. Stop watching violent and depressing movies and reading upsetting material. Why feed your mind negative information when you can nourish it with positive images and soothing experiences like beautiful art and classical music?

NATURAL FOODS FOR STAMINA:

Eating a diet without sugar, caffeine, and other toxic chemicals will not only keep you physically strong but will keep you emotionally strong as well. It will help prevent the mood swings and depression that are triggered by these kinds of foods. A healthy diet is the number one way to support your immune system.

Learn to avoid those "comfort foods" that are high in sugar and fat. Although they may produce a temporary feeling of well being, in the long run, they contribute to irritability and depression.

COUNSELING FOR CLARITY:

Often, a problem is just too overwhelming to deal with all by yourself. Don't ever feel like it's a weakness to seek help. A counselor's role is to help you identify and work through all of the mental and accompanying physical issues associated with serious problems.

When you are able to think more rationally and systematically, you are able to reach a speedier resolution to the problem. Then, you'll be able to restore your natural serenity.

It isn't always necessary to seek professional counseling. Often, just talking over the issue with your family or a trusted friend will help settle the turmoil inside of you. There is no comfort greater than the love and support from our loved ones.

EXERCISE FOR WELL BEING:

There is no medication on earth better than your own natural endorphins to lift the fog of depression and allow you to feel hopeful again.

When your body is in peak physical condition, you will possess the self-confidence and energy necessary to work through any problem.

. . . AND EMERGE BETTER THAN EVER

Any one of these actions, by itself, will be of benefit to you. But there is strength in numbers. So, by practicing all six in unison, you'll be assured of a more lasting success.

We will be exploring the Bounce plan in much further detail throughout this book. I will present specific situations and show you how to apply the steps to resolve the problem. I will discuss many ways of improving your diet, methods of exercise anybody can do, and positive mental exercises to help make your thinking clear and systematic. All of the steps act in unison and will put you on a path of emotional and physical healing.

There are no huge secrets here. Actually, you already know a lot of what I am going to tell you. But it's probably been put on the back burner of your mind. However, when we're through, you will see for yourself how incredibly effective all of these actions are when practiced together.

It is very empowering to know that there is nothing life can throw at you that you won't be able to handle. When you have the tools to bounce back, your confidence will soar along with your spirits and your life will work better than ever.

Part I: THE ISSUES

Illness:

Physical

CHAPTER 1

CANCER:
My Time At Bat

GROUND ZERO

I felt such a surge of relief during my eleventh routine breast cyst aspiration, when Dr. Mitchell Karlen extracted the yellow fluid from the scary lump and said, "Don't worry, Jan. It looks like just another cyst." The following morning, I happily removed the bandage and stepped into the shower.

As I soaped up my body, my fingers instinctively touched the spot on my right breast to feel the reassuring, flat-textured landscape. Instead, I felt the same lump that wasn't supposed to be there anymore.

Automatically, my mind went into denial thinking, "No, this can't be." I felt again. Sure enough—the lump. Not one time during the fifteen years that I had been having this procedure done, had this happened before. My heart started pounding, and my legs felt weak. So I stepped out of the shower, and dried off. I stood in front of the mirror, with the full morning sun shining on my right breast, and took a really close look. That's when I noticed the ever-so-slight difference in the texture of the skin on that breast from the other one.

My blood went cold. I knew this could be a sign of malignancy. The skin over the lump had what looked like very tiny stretch marks on it. I knew that dimpling of the skin could signal cancer.

I immediately dialed Dr. Karlen's office. His nurse said he was on vacation for two weeks. I scheduled the earliest appointment I could, and then, waited and worried. . .waited and worried. My fingers felt that lump thousands of times, each time hoping it would just mysteriously be gone. But no such luck.

On The Lighter Side

Wouldn't you know it? Every time you need a doctor, he's either on vacation, on the golf course, or doing both—in Hawaii.

BIOPSY

On December 15, 1997, my dad's eightieth birthday, Dr. Karlen performed a breast biopsy under a local anesthetic. I was mildly nervous, but mostly relieved to be getting it taken care of. Even with the knowledge of the skin changes, I still believed it was going to be benign. Another cruise on De Nile, huh?

Dr. Karlen's nurse, Kathy, was upbeat. She said not to worry, that the odds were in my favor. They had been having a great stretch all morning. All four biopsies they had done turned out to be benign. So, as Dr. Karlen began the surgery, we were both optimistic. We even told each other a few jokes during the first few minutes. But, as the time went on, he became more and more quiet—which unsettled me. I tried to calm myself by thinking, "He's just engrossed in this procedure—don't jump to any wild conclusions."

However, when I heard him say to the nurse, "This has to go for a frozen section," I couldn't remain in denial any longer. I knew he had a strong suspicion it was malignant. He said, "Jan, the tumor has a hard center. That indicates either scar tissue or malignancy. The odds are 50/50."

After he closed up the incision, nurse Kathy helped me sit up, and gave me some orange juice. Dr. Karlen said to come back to the office in two hours, when the result of the frozen section would be back from pathology.

On The Lighter Side

When I heard those lousy odds, the first thing that crossed my mind was, what happened to Kathy's story about the "odds being in my favor"? Heck, I wouldn't want her making any bets for me at the track!

THE LONG, DARK TUNNEL

Never in my life have I experienced the kind of overwhelming sense of doom that enveloped me. I ran from the office, down the hallway, feeling like I was in a long, dark tunnel. When I reached my husband, I could hardly get the words out: "My God, Mark. He thinks it's malignant."

We went back to our car in the parking garage. I sat there, emotionally frozen, for the next two hours. Everything around me seemed dim. It was like being in the bottom of a deep, dark well, unable to see daylight. I was so frightened, I couldn't even cry. My mind raced. I pictured myself bald and emaciated from chemo. I thought about lying in a hospital bed with my life slipping away. I felt overwhelming sorrow for my children. My guts felt like they had been clubbed. The dread was staggering.

When the two hours were up, I literally had to force one foot in front of the other, just to walk back to the doctor's office. The minute I saw Dr. Karlen's face, I knew I hadn't dodged the bullet. He motioned for us to sit down. He told me I had lobular carcinoma. However, there was encouraging news. It was a small tumor, and in an early stage. Promising signs. Even though it had spread into the margin of the incision in two tiny areas, he said he was still "cautiously optimistic" there wouldn't be any further spread.

The next day, he removed ten lymph nodes from my right armpit, and removed a wider band of tissue around the original excision. This is called a "partial mastectomy." He had to see if the cancer had spread into any other areas.

CHAPTER 2

Getting A Grip:
The Stuff You're Made Of

REACHING INSIDE

A cancer diagnosis is the kind of experience that totally levels you. You quickly find out who you are and what you're made of. Sure, I was scared stiff. But I kept going over the positives in my mind. I had a stage one. I was not going to die. So, the minute I got home, I called my parents, my sister, and my two sons. I gave them all an optimistic report. I told them, "Don't worry. This is not going to kill me. I have an early stage, and I'll get it taken care of."

Even though I am a total social butterfly and dearly love all my girl-friends, I didn't call any of them with the news. Now was the time, if ever, when I needed to reach inside and find the strength to keep myself together. I instinctively knew that the telling and re-telling of the whole saga would drain too much of the precious energy I needed to get through the whole ordeal ahead of me.

Thanks to my six-day-a-week aerobics schedule, I physically sailed through the initial biopsy and partial mastectomy. But emotionally was another story. Let me tell you how much cancer humbles you. Driving back through the city, I saw homeless people and actually *envied* them. They didn't have cancer, but I did. That fact took away all of my feelings of control and profoundly shook my confidence. During the next three days while I waited for the pathology report, I stayed in the house, clinging to my familiar environment, while my fate spun out of control.

MORE UNCERTAINTY

A week later, I was back in Dr. Karlen's office, waiting for the pathology report. The moment of truth was here. I sat there, in my paper examination gown, shivering from cold and fear. When he appeared with the report in his hand, I felt like I was about to be executed by a firing squad. "The news is good," he announced. I felt a slight thawing of my muscles but was still braced for anything. "No lymph node involvement—all ten are clear. The tumor is small, but there is a slight involvement to the edge of the first margin."

My shoulders slumped. I was almost too afraid to ask, "What does that mean?"

He sighed, "I'd feel better if you saw a surgeon and oncologist to discuss the possibility of a mastectomy. I want to make sure I didn't leave any cancer cells behind."

Geez Louise. The Lord giveth, and the Lord taketh away.

Once again, I sat there in stunned silence. My mind was racing with these thoughts: "Oh, isn't this great? Why can't I ever catch a break? I thought I could get away with lumpectomy and radiation, but I guess not. Why does my case always have to be so iffy?"

In a few short seconds, I went from elation to depression. But no matter how depressed I felt, I knew I didn't have the luxury of wallowing in it. Dr. Karlen said I had an 85 percent chance of survival if I did the right thing. He immediately called both an oncologist and a reconstructive surgeon. I took the first available appointments with each of them.

DECISION TIME

On December 29, 1997, I met with the two doctors. Both were at the top of their respective fields, and both were incredibly compassionate. The oncologist was a beautiful young woman named Dr. Philomena McAndrew. First, she explained about the kind of cancer I had and the treatment options. Then, she performed a physical examination. Afterwards, she hugged me. Let me tell you something. That one small gesture allowed me to stop feeling like a leper. It did wonders to assuage my feelings of isolation. It was so comforting to know I had a powerful ally at my side, fighting this hideous enemy.

The reconstructive surgeon's appointment proved to be the one that allowed me to decide which course of treatment to take. I checked in at the desk with Dr. Tearston's office manager, Vicki. She was this adorable, perky gal, with a dynamite shape. I couldn't help but feel a pang of jealousy, because I thought I was going to lose mine.

To my surprise, she appeared again when the doctor was examining me. At first, I didn't know why she had come into the room. But it soon became wonderfully clear. Seven years before, Dr. Tearston had reconstructed one of her breasts. She was only forty-two when she was diagnosed with breast cancer. Her reconstructed breast was phenomenal looking. It was reconstructed from the fat in her stomach and was so perfect looking, there was no visible difference from her other breast.

One big factor kept echoing in my mind. Dr. McAndrew had explained that lobular cancer tends to be multi-focal. This meant that I had *up to* a 20 percent chance of it recurring in the other breast. Yikes. I knew I didn't want to live with the kind of immobilizing fear that the "other shoe" was going to drop in one year or ten years. Being fibrocystic, I didn't want to live with my hand on my left breast, fighting hysteria every time a cyst, a pain, or anything else occurred. That would ruin my quality of life.

Still, another consideration was that the reconstructed breast would be higher and perkier looking than the existing one. So, my left breast would need to have a surgical procedure (maxopexy), to make both breasts the same level on the chest. If I did decide to have the non-cancerous breast removed as a prophylactic measure, I'd get more of a "matched set." But, wait, there's more. They said my nipples had to be reconstructed and tattooed at a later time. And—that would cost extra! That was the first laugh I had since the ordeal began.

Dr. Tearston said the skin on my breasts was intact and flexible enough to do both implants without using expanders. These are devices that stretch the skin over the course of weeks or months to accommodate the implant. But, thanks to his skill, I was going to be able to bypass that process and return to a 36C immediately after surgery. That did it for me. Case closed. I decided, then and there, to have bilateral mastectomies with immediate reconstruction. My decision was made with a clear head, sound medical knowledge, and a complete faith in my doctor's ability. And I have never regretted taking this course. To the contrary, I believe it was the smartest thing I've ever done.

On The Lighter Side

I figured oh well, join the crowd. Everyone in L.A. has breast implants—it's the law. So, I might as well ask for the really big ones—the kind you need a building permit for.

I signed all the papers, and my surgery was scheduled for five weeks from that day. I needed that time to allow the partial mastectomy to heal and the swelling to go down under my arm.

But life goes on. Immediately after this consultation, I boarded a plane bound for New York City (with my chest bound), to appear on the *Today Show*. I was asked to roast Matt Lauer on the occasion of his fortieth birthday, with my book, *40: Deal With It*. I was thrilled. At that point, my philosophy was simple: You're either alive or you're dead. And I was very much alive. So I'd better start acting like a live person and enjoy every precious second that was given to me.

On The Lighter Side

It turned out that the double mastectomies were a piece of cake compared to the Matt Lauer interview! After I told a few jokes about his hairline receding after forty, he was visibly miffed. Two days later, he went on *The Rosie O'Donnell Show* and called me a "blond nut job." From the looks of his hair today, I obviously touched upon a "sensitive" area.

THE SURGERY

On Wednesday, January 22, 1998, at 2:30 pm, I underwent bilateral mastectomies with immediate reconstruction at Cedars Sinai Hospital in Los Angeles. I was a nervous wreck, but a cool thing happened. Walter Matthau was on the same elevator I was taking up to surgery. I have always totally adored him. So, for me, it was my lucky omen. I went into surgery with a smile on my face.

The surgery was certainly no walk in the park. But, it wasn't any nightmare experience, either. Physically, I was very strong from twenty-five years of exercising. So, the truth is that I pretty much sailed through the surgery.

Friday morning, a day and a half after surgery, I was discharged from the hospital. Mentally, I was set on healing and returning to normal as quickly as possible. In my opinion, waiting for the final biopsy report was more trying than the surgery. It would reveal if there were any residual cancer left and whether I would require any adjuvant treatment, such as chemotherapy.

For the next week, I jumped every time the phone rang. When Dr. McAndrew finally called, my hand shook as I held the receiver. But her news sent my spirits through the roof. No residual cancer in the breast that had the tumor. No new cancer present in the other breast. There was a cystic area, but it was benign. The tumor was under one centimeter and not particularly aggressive. Chemo was not necessary.

My tumor was "estrogen dependent," which means that it grows in the presence of estrogen. So, Dr. McAndrew prescribed Tamoxifen for the next five years. Tamoxifen is an anti-estrogen pill that cuts down the chances of recurrence by 50 percent. That put me into the 93 percent survival category. Can't beat those odds.

For the first time since my ordeal began, my body relaxed enough for me to weep. The gratitude I felt toward God and my surgeons was awesome.

But, even with all the good news, I know there are no 100 percent guarantees. There is always the small possibility that the cancer might pop up again, even decades after the first bout. That uncertainty is both a curse and a blessing. The blessing: Cancer survivors learn to treasure every day and take little for granted. The curse: We have to learn how to make peace with the knowledge that there's a chance the cancer could return at any time. And, the next time, we might not be so lucky.

Sure, it sucks. But we've got no choice. We've got to play the hand we've been dealt. As time goes on, we're better able to compartmentalize this worry. With each passing year, the fear gets dimmer and dimmer.

CHAPTER 3

Healing:
How I Bounced Back

CANCER ATTACKS ON TWO MORE LEVELS

When I heard the words, "you have breast cancer," it scared me beyond belief. The fear I felt became crippling. Cancer destroys confidence like it destroys healthy tissue. I learned firsthand that it's normal to feel like you have lost all control over the rest of your life—or to question if you will even have one. I experienced emotions that manifested themselves first as fear, then anger, then depression.

The fact is that after the initial diagnosis, you need a clear head and intelligent plan of action to wage war on this insidious enemy. That's where a "dress rehearsal" can save your life. When you familiarize yourself with the types of breast cancer, the stages it progresses through, and the medical treatments recommended at each stage, you're way ahead of the game. More often than the disease, it's the denial that kills the patient.

When we unexpectedly have to face our own mortality, it shakes us to our very foundations. I learned from my own experience that a spiritual foundation gave me the strength I needed for this battle.

Even though I am not a highly religious person, I instinctively turned inward. I used prayer and meditation to find my own center of strength. If I was going to successfully overcome this disease, I needed to calm my insides.

When you meditate, something amazing happens. You begin to understand from the depths of your being that you are not merely flesh, bone, and brain cells. Who we really are transcends the physical body. We have a consciousness, a life of the soul, that will continue on after the body is gone. When you are able to really internalize this concept, everything changes for the better. Your position shifts from the storm into its calm eye.

Today, I'm in the happiest place I've ever been, and I'm going to share with you how I got here. It is my belief that the physical, emotional, and spiritual parts of us are interconnected, and each one has a profound effect on the other. Therefore, permanent healing can take place only when we work through our problem, on all three levels.

BOUNCING BACK

Physical Healing

A doctor can't make me healthy. That's my job. He can administer tests and monitor my body to see if a disease is present. But maintaining my health is up to me.

Here's a summary of what I learned, firsthand, from experience, reading resource books, and listening to experts.

Nutrition: I am convinced that nutrition is the key to maintaining good health. Later on, I'll discuss my personal nutrition plan in detail. But for now, I'll give you the main tenets of my nutritional philosophy.

The closer you get to nature in terms of eating foods grown without chemicals, the healthier you'll be. When you eat a well-balanced diet from nature, and not out of a box, you won't even need vitamin supplements.

I try to buy only organically grown fruits and vegetables. Pesticides are toxic. Nobody really knows how carcinogenic they are. After having cancer, I figure the last thing my body needs is to be exposed to any kind of carcinogen.

On The Lighter Side

I get a big kick checking out the various farmers' markets in town. It's like taking a step back in time to the sixties, seeing the people milling about in their Birkenstocks, tie-dye T's, and Willie Nelson braids and headbands.

I make sure I have eight glasses of water every day. The saying is: By the time you're thirsty, you're already dehydrated. Water plays a crucial role in keeping the body's immune system healthy. It's also the vehicle by which we rid toxins from our body.

Exercise: It goes hand in hand with proper nutrition in maintaining a healthy immune system. When you exercise, your circulation works to the max, bringing blood to every organ in the body. It also helps to remove toxins through perspiration, with the added benefit of lowering your blood pressure.

I take kickboxing and aerobics classes six times a week. My skin glows after exercising. Often, I'm the oldest person in the class. But so what? I don't put limits on myself. Why? Because nobody told me I couldn't do it.

My exercise regimen not only allowed me to sail through my surgeries but also helped me to heal quickly. I had no lymphedema (swelling of the lymph glands) under my arms after the mastectomies. I experienced a minimum of pain, and was driving my car a week after surgery. I was back on the treadmill in three weeks, and back to the gym, full time, in three months.

I have always held the belief that exercise is a major factor that will help my body prevent a recurrence of cancer. Exercise not only makes me feel great, but protected, too. Cancer cells do not like oxygen. It puffs them up, and they become more susceptible to being detected and destroyed by white blood cells. Recently, my belief was validated by a new medical study I first read about in the L.A. Daily news. Subsequently, I have seen it printed in quite a few magazines. It says that breast cancer recurrence rates are not only dramatically reduced by exercising but also reduced proportionately to the number of days you exercise.

Spiritual Healing

When your external world is rocked, you must go inward to gain a sense of peace. I accomplished this through meditation. After my diagnosis, I would sit out in the sunshine in my beautiful backyard, with its flowers and palm trees, meditating for thirty minutes each day. It cleared the "chatter" from my head and engulfed me with a sense of peace.

Sunshine is good for you. I am not advocating going out there and frying yourself to a crisp, but even thirty minutes a day helps your body make vitamin D, which lowers your cholesterol. Sunshine also has anti-tumor properties. There have been studies that show women who get a regular amount of sunshine have a lower incidence of breast cancer.

On the Lighter Side

I remember my high school days, back in the Pleistocene Era, when I would slather myself in baby oil and iodine, surround my body with a reflective foil blanket, and then go out and fry in the sun in my backyard. Good grief! By the end of the summer, it was a wonder that I didn't have to be identified by my dental records!

Every day, I listen to audiotapes of some wonderful spiritual teachers like Dr. Wayne Dyer, Deepak Chopra, and Louise Hay. They all espouse the same incredibly comforting philosophy:

We are more than our bodies, our brains, and our ego. Our consciousness transcends that. We are spirit. And when the physical body dies, our consciousness and spirit will go on.

It took me about a year to really "get" this concept. But once I was able to incorporate it into my heart, my fear of death started to ebb away. It gave me a whole new perspective on life, and my purpose in it. When you believe that the soul goes on to a more loving plane, you no longer view death as your enemy.

MY SPIRITUAL TEACHERS

There is a saying: "When the pupil is ready, the teacher will appear." This happened for me in a most unusual way. Right after my surgery, it was hard for me to sleep at night. So, I would put on my headset and listen to the radio. One night, I happened to hear a female doctor and breast cancer survivor talking about her experience on a radio program. Dr. Lorraine Day is an orthopedic surgeon from California who battled and won her war against an eleven-pound breast tumor. She did it with a lumpectomy, followed by her own tailor-made program of nutrition and meditation. And it worked! She has been cancer-free for more than ten years.

She said that when a person's immune system is functioning properly, the T-cells kill off bacteria, viruses, and even cancer cells. However, the T-cell count decreases in response to stress and improper nutrition. Dr. Day believed if she could get her immune system back to working optimally, it would destroy the remaining cancer cells and save her life. But her cancer was advanced, and she was very sick. She had to act quickly.

She started juicing pounds and pounds of yellow and green vegetables, extracting the necessary vitamins and minerals to heal her body. She began drinking a lot of water. It took about eighteen months to reverse her cancer, but she did it. She actually beat cancer without radiation or chemotherapy. She made a series of videos, explaining the steps she took to get well. I immediately sent for them, and began following her program.

Emotionally, this put me back on track. I felt like I was on the right path and I would be able to put the cancer behind me. I was learning how to live in the "now," focusing on each day and not worrying about the next. My spiritual healing opened the door for emotional and physical healing.

I knew my spiritual door was opening the day I met Louise Hay, one of my favorite authors, in person. I happened to be attending a yearly convention for booksellers, authors, and people in the book trade. This particular year, it was being held in Los Angeles. When I spotted Louise Hay in the Hay House booth, I excitedly went over and introduced myself. I told her that I was a cancer survivor and had been listening to her tapes for two years. I told her how helpful they were in getting me through the trying days after my cancer diagnosis. She looked directly into my eyes, smiled her dazzling smile, and said to me: "Jan, your cancer is behind you. It's part of your past." That was her wonderful way of telling me that I shouldn't define myself by this disease. In her words, "It's over and done with."

Emotional Healing

Although I would certainly advocate attending a cancer support group for anybody else, I didn't feel the need to go myself. Because my cancer was diagnosed at an early stage, I did not have to go through debilitating chemotherapy or face an uphill battle to survive. I was strong and was able to return to a normal life so quickly, I never felt depressed.

I also believe in the immense healing and restorative power of laughter. Being the author of more than twenty humor books, I figured now was the time to start practicing what I'd been preaching for years. So, as part of my healing process, my husband and I began going to the Improv Comedy Club every weekend. I also watched every funny show that was on TV.

The physical act of laughing releases endorphins in the body, the same way exercise does. So, besides strengthening my immune system, the laughter helped me to put my problems in a proper perspective.

On The Lighter Side

After seven years of attending the famous Improv Comedy Club in L.A., I can recite all the routines of the best stand-ups in America. Now everybody thinks that I'm such a riot, I get invited to all the best parties in town!

MY MISSION

After about a year, it became apparent to me that I needed to go out and speak to women about my breast cancer experience. I started giving a speech about how I faced and overcame cancer, stressing all the positive things that came out of the experience. My goal is to eliminate the fear and dread that keeps women in denial and away from a quicker diagnosis. This has become my mission. I want every woman out there to know that an early diagnosis will not only ensure her survival but also allow her to regain her life in a very short time.

As more time elapses, the fear of having a recurrence grows dimmer in my mind. But, through my meditations, I have had the revelation that if I ever did suffer a recurrence, the worst thing would be to die knowing I hadn't done everything possible to keep myself healthy.

Let's face it—we're all going to die some day. But dying with a bunch of regrets is, to me, the worst way to go.

I have come to terms with the fact that death is an inevitable part of life. It is not a tragedy. The tragedy is a life that has been squandered or spent unfulfilled, without love.

I'M BACK!

These steps and principles can be applied to any illness, not only cancer. The truth is that we all have to face getting some kind of disease in our lifetimes. It might be diabetes, heart disease, a neurological disease, or something else. The good news is that this plan works to help you to rise above any of them.

I have bounced back—with a vengeance. My blood pressure is 110/70, my cholesterol is 165, and I weigh 118 pounds, the same weight I was at twenty-five. I hardly ever get sick with a cold, flu, or even a headache. My life is ten times better after the cancer than it was before.

Since having cancer, I try not to take anything for granted. It has helped me to realize just how much I love and cherish my life. Now, I am always trying to do everything I can to protect and maintain it. All the things I talked about will also help you to do a lot more than just get *through* a trauma. You'll be able to bounce back, just as I did, better than ever.

The Spiritual:

Loss

CHAPTER 4

Death Of A Loved One:
Healing the Heart

THE SUM OF ALL FEARS

We all live with the fear of someday losing our parents, a friend, or other family members. But the moment one of those uncomfortable thoughts creeps in, we automatically push it to the back of our minds. It seems like in our culture, especially, we haven't learned to deal very well with death or any other kinds of losses. We're programmed to believe that we will live to a ripe old age, and we consciously avoid thoughts about our own mortality or anyone else's. For us, death is the enemy.

Although this kind of thinking may be easier in the short run, it makes coping with death even harder. Like it or not, we're going to be faced with loss many times over before we pass on. And the only way we can keep from being permanently crippled by loss is by changing the way we think about it. Like illness, it's another one of life's traumas that we need to heal from.

My mother died in July 2001, and although it was terribly sad, I was able to cope with her death from many of the lessons my breast cancer had taught me. I'd like to share some of those lessons with you.

DEATH: A NATURAL TRANSITION

In order to cope with death, we have to come to terms in our hearts that death is a *natural* process, not a punishment. Like birth, it is a part of life that happens to everyone. We will need to change our old ways of thinking that categorize death as horrific, and the *worst* thing that can happen to a person. Death is not punitive. It's a natural occurrence that will eventually get around to both you and me.

When we learn to accept our own mortality, we can accept it more easily in others. Yes, death is sad and even tragic, in many cases. But it is *not* God's way of punishing us because we weren't good people.

GRIEF IS GOOD

When we lose someone we love, it's a lot easier to accept if we allow ourselves to grieve. If we are not able to grieve, it's almost impossible to move on.

A person who has trouble accepting the death of a loved one may try to block out his emotional pain with pills, or alcohol or by throwing himself into his work. Although this plan may work temporarily, trust me, it eventually catches up with you. You may go along for a time, seemingly in control of your emotions, and then when you least expect it—bam! The grief surfaces as *depression, anger,* or *illness.*

So, if you lose someone, it's important to accept that he is physically gone forever. The only way you can fully comprehend this reality is by allowing yourself to grieve. We have to experience sorrow before we can release it. It's very important to our own healing process to experience the sadness and not block it out with distractive or even destructive behavior. Don't go down that path. If you do, you'll never be able to heal completely.

Even two years after my mother's death, I might be looking at a photo or listening to a song, and tears well up out of nowhere. This is okay. It's normal. I don't fight it. I just go with it and experience the sadness. When I let myself do this, the occurrences lessen over time.

On The Lighter Side

As time passes, I am beginning to remember more and more of the funny quotes from my mother. At the end of her life when she was in the hospital, she pointed to a picture hanging on the wall and said to my brother, "Who is that?" He replied, "Mom, that's Jesus." She nonchalantly replied, "Oh, no wonder I didn't recognize him."

Often, we become the survivors who need to give strength and encouragement to other family members. For this task, you need to place your focus outside of yourself. You can't help anyone else if you're self-anesthetized with drugs. By being less self-absorbed and helping others with their grief, you can become part of the healing process.

BELIEF SYSTEMS

I was raised in the Catholic faith, and we attended mass every Sunday. But as the years have gone by, I stopped going to the physical place called "church" and began to adopt parts of all faiths into my beliefs. Through experience, I have come to understand that we are more than just physical beings. We all have a soul that will survive the physical body and go on forever. This kind of thinking will help a person cope with death better than anything else. Whether we come by these beliefs through organized religion or by other paths, it doesn't matter. They allow your life to make more sense and have greater meaning. I've always found that people with strong spiritual beliefs are able to overcome the bumps of life with a lot more ease than those who believe in nothing.

When a person believes that this life is just one plane of many that go on eternally, then death isn't such a horrific event. If we believe that some day, our spirits will all be united after death, then life itself makes more sense. The death of an elderly parent is always hard, but the death of a child or an unexpected death from an accident is the kind that is incredibly brutal to deal with emotionally. Trying to find the meaning of why some poor child is suffering horribly with terminal cancer has to be the hardest thing on earth to understand or accept. But a strong belief in God helps people cope with the most seemingly cruel or senseless deaths. This is where religion supplies many of the answers that mortal man just cannot.

I will always remember Rose Kennedy's reaction to the death of her second son, John F. Kennedy. She said, "I will not be vanquished." Rose was comforted by her incredibly strong faith in God. She went on to honor her son's memory by leading an exemplary life, giving to others as well as her own family. She obviously believed it was God's plan and that she would be united with her children again in the next life.

The eastern philosophies of life and death provide a different point of view and answer many of the questions that we westerners have a hard time understanding. After reading many books about eastern spiritual beliefs, I found I was better able to cope with death and loss. They believe that we have eternal souls that keep coming back to the physical plane, i.e. reincarnating, until all our lessons have been learned. At the ultimate point of being enlightened, our souls will join with our creator forever. I find that these philosophies expand the mind and give comfort to us westerners who are apt to be grounded in the one-dimensional, physical way we view life.

SELF-SUPPORT

During a stressful time, just like during an illness, we need to take special care of ourselves. We have to come to terms with the fact that nothing will ever bring a loved one back. But we are still here, and we still have a wonderful life ahead of us. Life *is* for the living. Therefore, we must take care not to sabotage ourselves out of misplaced anger or unexpressed grief. We can honor the memory of the dead person best by living out a productive, happy life.

We can be an inspiration to our children by showing them how dear we hold our own lives, by taking care of our bodies during a crisis. When the physical body is strong and healthy, it is a lot easier for the psyche to bounce back from any traumatic event.

COPING WITH LOSS

The following are some helpful things that I have learned from my own experience of coping with loss. They will help you not only navigate through your crises, but bounce back a lot quicker and more completely.

Prepare For the Inevitable:

The most important lesson I learned from my mother's death was this: *It's a lot easier to work through your grief if you have no regrets about how you treated loved ones when they were alive.* We must strive to do this, because as you know, there's no chance of it happening after they are gone. Then, when the loved one passes on, letting go is a lot less painful when we let go with love. Trust me on this.

In a way, I was fortunate that my mother didn't die suddenly. She had been in progressively worse health for five years before she actually passed on. My mom and dad lived three thousand miles away, so our relationship was mostly phone calls and twice yearly visits.

Each time I visited my mom in the last few years of her life, she looked more and more debilitated. I'd always leave with my heart in my stomach, thinking it was the last time I'd ever see her. It made me acutely aware that I had to make every minute count. The time we had left together should be filled with kindness and laughter, not tension and resentment. Now, knowing my mother, this wasn't always easy! She was a real "party gal" who loved her cocktails and cigarettes.

She had a sharp wit and an even sharper tongue.

For years, I resented her drinking, her remarks that sometimes hurt, and her reluctance to visit any of us in the family. But, in her waning years, I realized I'd better lose my resentments fast and accept her unconditionally for who she was. I had to do this for my own well being as much as for hers. Was she flawed? Sure. But, who isn't? Who has June Cleaver for a mom anyway? Nobody. That kind of perfection exists only on TV.

Once I accepted my mom for the unique character that she was, we shared the best years of our mother/daughter life. I was sorry I hadn't done it years before I really knew her days were numbered. But *at least I did it.*

I called her every day from California, even for a few minutes. Even if she was pushing my buttons, I refused to lose my cool. Instead, I'd cheerily announce, "Mom, I have to go now." This avoided any impending confrontation. It was the wise thing to do. This way, when I called the next day, she was happy to hear from me, and I was happy to talk with her. There was no tension. I like to call it my *Alzheimer principle.* I immediately forget anything upsetting that was said.

Before I hung up, I began the practice of saying, "Love you, mom." I knew her Yankee guts were churning at this sentimentality, but she learned to be gracious about it. In fact, I believe that she secretly loved hearing it.

On her eighty-fifth birthday, I organized a family reunion at my folks' home in Connecticut. Mom was pretty much not walking anymore, and crotchety as hell, but I persevered. She protested that she` was too weak and not up for all the hoopla. She said that the great-grandkids would make her nervous. In her half-kidding/half-scolding way, she told me: "Jan, I know you're only doing this because you think I'm gonna die soon."

Ouch! She had such a way of nailing the truth. Maybe I was doing it for myself, but you know what? It didn't matter. We both reaped the benefits.

I kidded back, "Yeah, you're right. And we're coming whether you like it or not."

She loved it. She had the best time of her life. She actually kissed my husband goodbye when we left. Believe me, that was an event rarer than Haley's comet.

Because she was housebound, I made a practice of calling my mom from my cell phone, so she could live vicariously through me. I'd call her from the train and let her hear the whistle and the conductor's announcements. I'd call her from Hawaii and let her listen to the lovely guitar music being played poolside.

One week before she died, I called from Seattle to tell her about the birth of her fifth great-grandchild. She was pretty sharp and funny, joking about how my son was probably late getting his wife to the hospital. As usual, she was right!

The day before she died, my call found her in dire straits. She was having a horrible time breathing. She said, "I can't take much more of this, Jan. I want to go." And so, she did. She died peacefully in her sleep at eight o'clock the next night.

Celebrate Their Life When They're Still Living:

My brother, my sister, and I all worked hard at making the last years of our relationship with Mom close and happy ones. So, when she died, we were all able to let go with no regrets. We weren't devastated at her funeral. We were terribly sad but were at peace with her and with ourselves. We knew that she was in a far better place. Death is not always the worst thing that can happen to you. In my mom's case, it was a blessing.

It's a lot easier to work through grief *when we take the emphasis off of ourselves.* My mom was suffering, and the truth was that death must have been a welcome relief for her. When I focused on that, it made it a lot easier to bear.

We had a private funeral for her. In death she looked a lot better than she had in life. She looked really wonderful—and that was so comforting. For years before she died, she was always squawking about how she wanted a closed casket. At her funeral, we joked about how mad she'd be that we didn't comply with her wishes of having a closed casket. The truth is that she looked so darn beautiful we knew that she'd forgive us.

On The Lighter Side

For the last three years before she died, my mom was always scolding us "kids" (ages 66, 60, and 58), in her own inimitable way. She would say, "You kids better listen to me. I don't want an open coffin where all those damn people will be staring at me. So, if you're thinking about having a viewing, forget about it."

We celebrated her life at her funeral. Each of us got up and told a funny story about some memorable thing she had said or done. And, believe me, we didn't run out of anecdotes. On the last day of her life, Mom was scolding the nurse for exercising her legs. She said to her: "What in the hell are you bothering with that for? Can't you see I have one foot in the grave?" That was my mom. Cracking 'em like eggs right up until the end.

My brother told the best one of all, though. One I had never heard before. It captured the loving and playful side of my mother I had only wished I could have seen more of when she was alive. He said that when he was ten years old and she was walking him home from school in the snow, she suddenly fell to the ground, making "snow angels." She was laughing with delight, and it totally astounded him. That's an image I will carry with me until I join her in the next life. It's so comforting and beautiful.

Keep Them Alive After They Die:

Two days after my mom died, I was scheduled to give a speech at a "Girls Night Out" event in Los Angeles. At the end of my talk, I shared that I had just lost my mom and what a character she was. I told them some hilarious stories about the things she said and did over the years. And, to this day, I still do this every time I give a speech. I always will. It's my way of keeping her alive and close to me.

On The Lighter Side

My favorite story of all was in 1995 when Mom was in the E.R. being examined for a possible stroke. She was really impatient with all of the questions the doctor was asking, trying to assess her mental acuity. At one point, he asked her, "Who is the president of the United States?" She gruffly replied, "What are you asking me that for? Everyone knows it's Hilary."

My family is very open in talking about my mom. Often, when a person dies, others are afraid they may be "opening the wounds" by talking about them. This is an unfortunate misconception. Go ahead and talk. Talk all you want. It's very healing to the psyche and the soul.

I keep my mom alive in my thoughts by picturing her sitting next to me on a plane, in the car, or on my bed. I talk to her in my thoughts. She is always alive for me.

My Small Miracle

Three weeks after my mom passed away, she appeared to me in a dream. She looked healthy and seemed about sixty years old. She was sitting on the same couch she had been confined to for the latter part of her life. Mom was calm and talked to me in a serious tone. I instinctively knew that she was coming from a place of unconditional love. In life, my mom was funny, but she had a real cynical side too.

However, in the dream, that was completely gone and replaced by love and concern. She said that my dad was going to be terribly lonely and that she was worried about him. This kind of surprised me because she and my dad had their stormy moments right up until the end. She said she wanted me to send him beautiful cards, because they would comfort him and make him happy. After that, I knew she had to go. Her face dissolved into three younger faces, and then she disappeared.

I woke up knowing from every fiber of my being that she was not just a figment of my imagination. It was really her. That day, I went out and bought every card I could find. Cards of cheer, missing you cards—you name it, I bought it. To this day, I still send my dad one every day. And as usual, Mom was right. I had totally underestimated how hard he took her death. He was desperately lonely and grief-stricken that first year.

Dad kids me that he doesn't have time to be lonely because he's too busy opening up his cards! I tell him that I have to because I got explicit instructions from the "big boss." He loves it. I know my mom does, too.

COPING TIPS

The emotional trauma from a death can produce many of the same physiological effects as illness. It traumatizes the psyche and depresses the immune system. So, when we are suffering through a trauma, it's vitally important to pay close attention to our bodies. We need to take special care of ourselves through a good diet and plenty of exercise.

The natural endorphins from exercise will help lift depression better than any pill. Support your immune system with the same healthy diet we talked about in the chapter on illness. If you are having difficulty working through the grief on your own, don't be reluctant to seek counseling. Join a support system through grief counseling or by joining a grief workshop. It's an enormous help to share your feelings with others who are going through a similar loss.

To Sum Up:

- Death is a natural occurrence. It is not a punishment from God.
- Healing cannot take place when you attempt to numb your feelings with alcohol or drugs. Allow yourself to grieve.
- Having strong spiritual beliefs helps one to cope better with life, as well as death.
- Learning about or even embracing some of the eastern philosophies of death will expand your thinking and bring you comfort.
- It is vital to support the physical body when going through an emotional trauma. It helps the healing process to work faster and more permanently.
- Losing a loved one is less traumatic when you can let go with no regrets.
- Holding on to resentments retards the healing process. We must learn how to make peace with the person while he or she is still living.
- Celebrate your loved ones while they are still alive. Don't wait until they are too sick or far gone to benefit.
- Take the emphasis off yourself. When you focus on the suffering of the loved one, you may come to realize that death is sometimes a better alternative to living.
- You can keep your loved one alive in your thoughts. Don't be afraid to talk about them with others who loved them, too.

CHAPTER 5

Divorce:
Loving The Enemy

THE TRIFECTA OF UPSETS

Divorce is one of life's major traumas, touching more than fifty percent of those who marry. Unfortunately for me, I've been one of those statistics—twice. Believe me, in many ways, divorce is a lot tougher to work through and bounce back from than a loss from death.

Usually, with a death, the unresolved issues are laid to rest with the loved one. But with divorce, the issues remain alive and thrive on the fuel of discontent and are often thrown back in our faces, for years afterwards. If the parties remarry, then there are even more people with issues who regularly upset our lives. Peace becomes a rare commodity.

On The Lighter Side

Nowadays, with all the divorces, remarriages, and blended families going on, our family trees have more branches than Bank of America.

There's no question that divorce is one of the hardest things to bounce back from. But, it is *not* impossible. By applying the principles of the Bounce plan on a daily basis, you will have the necessary tools to work through each issue as it arises.

Divorce acts like an octopus that simultaneously upsets our physical, emotional, and spiritual equanimity. Therefore, in order to resolve problems on all three levels, it takes a solid commitment to adopt *and* practice the Bounce plan's principles as a new way of life.

SHIFT YOUR FOCUS

In order to maintain your equilibrium and remain positive during and after a divorce, it is crucial that you shift your attention away from the enemy (i.e., your spouse, et al.), and onto yourself.

Marriages end for all kinds of reasons, generating varied levels of pain, depression, and anger. A husband or wife may cheat on the other, arousing powerful feelings of anger and betrayal. Other times a marriage just seems to run its course, and feelings of love slowly wither away for both parties. There are also instances when this happens for only one spouse, whereas the other is still in love. The spouse that leaves this relationship often develops feelings of unbearable guilt, while the other grapples with tremendous anger and feelings of abandonment.

The most common and destructive mistake an injured party can make is using all of his or her energies to try and get even with the person who did the hurting. Here's the bad news. Revenge does not rebuild dignity or self-esteem. In fact, it gets you no place, except to add more unhappiness and upset to your life.

It's a given that divorce always hurts both parties in various ways and degrees. It generates a range of emotions for anyone experiencing it, including sadness, hurt, anger, jealousy, and guilt. But these feelings, albeit normal, are also the most self-destructive ones.

Negative emotions will eat your heart and your guts out. They will make your brain produce chemicals that will depress your immune system, wreaking havoc on your body. These brain chemicals can be the cause of crippling depression and may also pave the way for stress-related illnesses. These disorders rob us of the energy we'll need to work through and resolve our trauma. So, we're left with all the initial problems of the divorce, *plus* a host of new emotional and physical ones—and no energy to deal with them.

So, for the preservation of your mind and body, you must shift from your negative focus on the enemy to a positive one on yourself.

LOVE YOUR ENEMY, HEAL YOURSELF

By now, your minds are probably racing with thoughts like: "Just how do I accomplish this shift of focus? Is it possible to just magically forget all the hurt, anger, and depression I'm suffering? Do I just move on peacefully without a fight?"

Look, I'm not saying that a person shouldn't stand up for herself. Divorces can turn out to be unfair and cruel to people. It happens. But, here's the thing. Trying to right a wrong with negative behavior will, ultimately, make you lose everything and gain nothing. Why would you sacrifice your mental health and upset yourself further by choosing a destructive path of revenge? To what end? By getting five minutes of temporary satisfaction by hurting your spouse? What about guilt? Allowing it to rule your thoughts, causing sleepless nights and physical dysfunction, is also counterproductive. Think about it. There should be no question. The personal price you pay for this behavior is way too high for little or no payoff.

As unbelievable as it may seem, my answer is, yes, that you should move on peacefully, and roll over and die without a fight. If you don't, you're going to die little by little, not just in your body, but in your soul and your psyche as well. Continuing to fuel negative emotions takes a lot of energy. Harboring a host of negative feelings will weaken your body and mind to the point that you're going to be a sitting duck for serious disease.

How often have you heard about a man or woman who went through a vicious divorce and then was diagnosed with cancer or suffered a heart attack just a short time later? It's no coincidence. Negative emotions and long-term stress on the body are scientifically known to weaken the immune system, allowing various diseases to take hold.

It's no small task. Learning to love the enemy is the hardest thing a person can do. Maybe to actually *love* your enemy is nearly impossible; however, we still need to work toward that goal by learning how to *forgive*. And to accomplish this, we'll have to work on eliminating our hate and anger. Trust me on this. It is the only way to permanently heal your mind and body and move forward to build a better life.

IS THERE A MAGIC PILL?

I know you are wondering if there is some sort of magic pill that will get rid of these negative feelings. You're hurt, you're angry, and you would love to make him feel just like you do. I know exactly how you feel. I've been there, done that myself. And, although there is no magic pill, there *is* a way to lessen those feelings. You can do it by shifting all of your thoughts and energy into positive actions aimed at helping yourself. Forget the enemy. From now on, it's *all about you.*

On The Lighter Side

Besides, karma takes care of it for you. The best revenge for your ex-spouse happens when he remarries a girl much younger than himself who has no idea whatsoever who the Doobie Brothers, Jackie Gleason or F. Scott Fitzgerald are. (And couldn't care less.) It gets even better when he starts getting dragged out on weeknights to Ludacris and Black Eyed Peas concerts!

Give yourself the following pep talk every day:

I am going to give myself a brand new life with a whole new outlook. I deserve to be happy, healthy, and loved. I will not allow negative feelings to consume my body and soul and keep me from having a wonderful life.

Believe me. That new life is right there, within your reach. You can have it by practicing the principles of the Bounce plan every day.

Don't waste another precious second. Start right now!

PUTTING THE PLAN INTO ACTION

BE POSITIVE:

Affirmations do work. Begin each day by saying out loud to yourself: "I deserve a happy and loving life, free from stress and conflict. I have the power to create this for myself. My life can have this and *anything else* I choose to have in it."

Remind yourself, daily, that your old situation did not work. It was negative, and it was hurting you. But, now you have the opportunity to begin anew and *the tools* to remain in the zone of happiness and well-being. Positive thoughts have a lot of power.

OVERCOME STRESS:

Divorce is, no doubt, one of the most stressful events in a person's life. You must constantly work to remove that stress and do the necessary work to stop perpetuating it. You must *not* contribute negative thoughts and actions that keep the stress ongoing.

Keep reminding yourself that negative emotions are killers. Stress feeds on jealousy and revenge, and can eventually manifest itself physically in monstrous forms, such as cancer and heart disease. Remember, only you have the power to *not* let that happen.

The quicker you get through the divorce, the quicker you will put the stress behind you. Even if it takes physically moving to another location, do it. It's your life we're talking about here. Your program for self-preservation is to take all actions that *support yourself.* Any energy aimed at your ex is energy you are taking away from your own healing process. Why give your precious energy away?

UPLIFT YOURSELF:

The old saying "misery loves company" is totally true. You will find that out, especially, when going through a divorce. A lot of unhappy people will flock to your side and dispense their "helpful" advice. So be on guard. Avoid these *energy vampires*. People who love to hear themselves talk are people who haven't worked through their own problems. They are stuck in the same old, unproductive, self-defeating behavior.

Don't waste your precious time on them. Their advice will not help you. Instead, they will repeatedly bring you down. Take charge of your situation by surrounding yourself exclusively with emotionally healthy people who truly care about you, people who can support you, encourage you, and help you move ahead with positive actions.

NATURAL FOODS AND EXERCISE:

I've combined these two because they work hand-in-hand. During a stressful divorce, it is imperative that you nourish and exercise your body. Begin treating your body like the temple it is.

A natural, healthy diet is crucial to maintain good health and the feeling of well-being. When we are feeling strong, we are much better able to handle our big problems successfully. When we are hungry or undernourished, our moods will be volatile, and we will feel like there's a big, empty pit in our stomachs. We will have the urge to fill that emotional hole with sugars and other comfort foods. Or we may substitute coffee and cigarettes for our meals, because we feel too "uptight" to eat. Red flag. *Do not* get on this self-destructive bandwagon.

Your body is already under attack from stress. You must go on the counterattack with a healthy diet and an exercise regimen that supports your immune system. Besides, now is the perfect time to begin looking and feeling your best, because you are starting a new and exciting life—a life in which you're the director for a change.

As far as exercise goes, I cannot say this enough:

There is no pill on earth that will help lift depression, eliminate anxiety, and promote a sense of well-being like the natural endorphins produced during exercise.

You will require a lot of physical strength to get through a divorce. No matter how depressed, anxious, or angry I am when I enter the gym, I always leave feeling happy, calm, and like I could take on the world! And, besides gaining strength, you'll want to look great. Lucky for you, the side effects of regular exercise are a toned, youthful, and slim body. As I always say, "Exercise is the best revenge!"

On The Lighter Side

There is no better way of working off anger than through rigorous exercise. I wrote about this in *Red Hot Mamas*, when I spoke of my power-boxing regimen. Every time my gloved hand hits that bag, I say: "This is for the telemarketers! This one's for my husband's ex! And this is for her attorney!" Aaaaah—I feel great!

COUNSELING:

Personally, I believe that counseling is a *must* during a divorce. Girlfriends, siblings, and parents are all helpful to talk to, but they lack *objectivity*. You will need an independent, unbiased voice to help you navigate through overwhelming issues.

Counseling will allow you to systematically sort through the myriad emotions you are feeling and help you to gain a better perspective. This, in turn, will allow you to work through those tough issues more effectively. Counseling will help you heal your ego, which has taken quite a bruising. Remember, you have to focus *on yourself* from now on. Forget about your what your ex spouse is doing. It's all about you, and how to maintain your physical, emotional, and spiritual health.

Counseling should be used in conjunction with the other tools listed in the Bounce plan. They all work *synergistically* to put you on the road to well-being and happiness. I promise you will emerge healthier and happier than ever before. And, when you practice the Bounce plan daily and use the given tools, well-being and happiness will always be a part of you!

To Sum Up

- In order to achieve permanent emotional, physical, and spiritual healing, you must shift all of your negative energy off of the enemy and put the positive focus on yourself.
- Negative feelings cause the brain to produce chemicals that depress the normal functioning of the immune system.
- When the immune system is compromised from long-term stress,

the body is more susceptible to serious diseases such as cancer, stroke, and heart attacks.

- Forgiveness is *the* key to healing. Always work toward the goal of learning to love the enemy.
- Using one's energy to get revenge is counterproductive. Use your energy to build a better life for yourself.
- One of the most effective ways to work off anger is with regular exercise.
- Positive thoughts have a lot of power. Saying positive affirmations every day will attract those things into your life.
- Do not take the advice of negative-thinking people. Surround yourself with positive people who love you and will help you work toward a happier life.
- Besides strengthening the immune system, natural endorphins produced during exercise will lift depression and give you a sense of well-being.
- Friends and family members are good to talk with, but they *lack objectivity*. A professional counselor will help you deal with the overwhelming issues more efficiently and effectively.

CHAPTER 6

Empty Nest:
Your Time to Fly

FLOWN THE COOP!

I'll never forget when my son left home for college. We went through the mandatory chaotic month before, getting his clothes packed, buying supplies for his dorm room, and all the rest of the pre-college preps. I was so preoccupied I didn't have time to think about how his leaving would affect me. About a week after he was gone, I was standing in my bedroom folding clothes, when it suddenly hit me like a ton of bricks! This was it. He was going to be on his own, for good. Sure, I'd see him on holidays, and maybe even summers, if I got lucky. But, he had begun his journey as an adult, without me at his side.

Who me? I'm not a crier. I didn't cry even when I was diagnosed with breast cancer. But. . .this? It literally brought me to my knees. I flung myself across the bed and sobbed my heart out for an hour. Then, I went into the shower and sobbed some more, as the pulsating spray fell on my face along with my tears. I finally got out, toweled off, and stopped crying. But, I stayed in one heck of a funk for the next week.

I spent the week reflecting about my son and the wonderful

moments we shared from the day he was born. I played those tapes over and over in my mind. This is the kind of loss where you experience a whole gamut of emotions, from joy to self-pity:

REGRET:
You review your life as a parent and inevitably come up with all kinds of regrets about the things you should have done.

INADEQUACY:
You feel like your usefulness is over and you're about to be sent out to pasture.

FEAR:
You get scared, wondering how you're going to be able to fill that empty hole in your life and your heart.

SADNESS:
You're disappointed with yourself for not spending more quality time together.

ANGER:
You're a bit miffed with your kid because he seems *way too happy* about leaving home and moving on.

On the Lighter Side

And why not? The day we moved Phil into his college dorm, I couldn't believe this was supposed to be an institution for higher learning! Besides his dorm being co-ed *and* having a pool, there were dozens of blonde bombshells clad in Daisy Duke cut-offs and teeny tiny T-shirts, bouncing all over the place. Phil's eyes were as big as saucers, and he had a robotic grin plastered across his face all afternoon. I thought to myself, "Is this college or *Baywatch*?"

. . .All this, plus much, much more. And, you know what? They're all normal feelings, shared by every other mom and dad on the planet. One of life's biggest transitions takes place when our kids are no longer under our roofs. Once we accept that, it's time to move on with the business of our own lives.

The fact is that this transition allows us to re-examine our roles in our changing lives. If we are already working, this might be the perfect time to take on more responsibility in our jobs, or even change to a whole new field. If we are stay-at-home moms, we can now think about beginning a career in the workplace. Or if we choose to remain at home, we might decide what new directions we can explore.

GET A LIFE

Some of us make the transition a lot easier than others. Women, especially, have a hard time letting go. In fact, I have a friend who actually stayed in a hotel near campus for the first month her daughter was in college. My friend justified being there by saying she could help her daughter make a "smoother transition" into college.

Oh, sure. I think we'd all agree that it was the mother, not the daughter, who was having trouble with the transition. Her behavior was a lot more *about her own needs* and not her kid's. There are parents who react radically because they're terrified of facing a life where they are no longer able to:

1. Control their kid.
2. Live their kid's life.

The parent owns this problem. And the saddest thing is that it's hurting the child. This kind of self-serving, dysfunctional behavior will only retard the young adult's transition into self-reliance. Granted, my friend's reaction was extreme. But, there are parents who obsess in different ways, and they need to get their own lives, asap.

This behavior is really *about control*, specifically, the unwillingness to give it up. There are a few facts of life that we must internalize before we can successfully let go:

1. Part of reaching adulthood is becoming autonomous from the parents. A young adult will be entering the phase in his life where he will become totally responsible for himself, making all of his own decisions.

2. As the parents of young adults, our role is to keep exerting a positive influence and giving guidance through example. But, by eighteen years of age, it's time to relinquish the reins of control and hand them over to your young adult.

3. You must trust that you have done the best job you know how to give your child the guidance, the moral foundation, and the love he needs to have a fulfilling and meaningful life. Now it's time to let go.

SPREAD YOUR WINGS

Life is an ongoing process for adults, not just for kids. It is still unfolding for everybody, at any age. Adults should never stop creating new and exciting horizons in their own lives. So now's a perfect time to take a good, objective look at your own life. Ask yourself the following questions:

Who am I, and what is my role in life?

Do I have another passion besides parenting?

When I am no longer parenting on a daily basis, what will make me happy?

What can I do that will make me feel productive?

If you find that you have absolutely no answers to any of these questions, there's no doubt you're going to have trouble moving on and getting past that empty nest.

HOW TO GAIN A NEW PERSPECTIVE

As human beings, we deserve and are supposed to have happy, fulfilled lives. Our role has never been just to be parents. We are also spouses, professionals, care takers for our own parents, artists, business people, and any number of other things. For those who have been limiting their thinking to define themselves solely as parents, it's time to think multidimensionally. No matter how noble parenting is, it is certainly not the only *worthwhile* role in life. You can be a parent *and* so much more.

Every one of us was given the ability to keep creating wonderful lives for ourselves, at every age. Our path is strictly our own. It is not our kid's, or husband's, or boss's. Our path in life is created and fulfilled by us alone. So, if we are unhappy or unfulfilled, only *we* can change that. It is totally possible, too. We have the power to do it.

LEARNING TO FLY

The main reason I was able to work through my empty nest so quickly was because at the same time my son was leaving, my first book got published. It was the most exciting thing that had ever happened to me. So even though I was losing my career as a parent of eighteen years, I was embarking on a whole new one as an author. That really made me happy, and fulfilled me on multiple levels:

1. It sparked my creativity.
2. It gave me a plan for MY future.
3. It gave me an incentive to work on staying healthy and keep up my stamina for a demanding career ahead.
4. It gave me a reason to get out of bed and goals to accomplish every day.
5. It allowed me to feel in control of my own life.
6. It made my self-esteem soar.
7. It gave me an opportunity to travel and meet new people,

broadening my outlook beyond my backyard.

8. It presented me with new challenges like deadlines, and forced me to use my brain again.

9. It presented me with the opportunity to learn about many new subjects that I researched for my books.

10. It gave me my own identity. I was not just somebody's mom, wife, or child. I felt important just being *me*.

On the Lighter Side

Oops. The heck with all the lofty stuff. I forgot to mention the most important thing—I was also making my own money for the first time in twenty years! Helloooo. There is no better way of fueling your independence than with the high-grade octane from your own bank account!

I can't emphasize the power of number ten enough. When you feel like you are making a significant contribution with your talents, it gives such a boost to your self-esteem. It allows you to shift your perspective, so that you see yourself as strong, independent, and worthy.

THE WIND BENEATH MY WINGS

Another important shift for me took place after my ordeal with breast cancer. That's when I became a public speaker. I not only wrote about my experience in books, but I started speaking about it, too.

I decided to start speaking because I wanted to reach out to women on a very personal level. I wanted allay their fears and spread the news that breast cancer is no longer the death sentence it was in our mothers' day.

The first time I was asked if I had ever done public speaking, I said "Sure!" (Well, *technically* I did—when I stood in front of a classroom for six years.) Was I scared about the prospect of speaking in front of five hundred adults? You bet! But, I shifted my perspective from *victim* to *survivor*. I thought, "Heck, if I could survive cancer, what's the big deal about talking to an audience?"

Since beating cancer, honestly, nothing much scares me anymore. Or if it does, it's not for very long. I am a much more adventurous person, now that I have been given back a life to be adventurous in! Besides, I have gained a burning passion to help women by relating my experience to them. It will be my mission for the rest of my life. I was able to replace my passion for parenting with a passion for writing and speaking. My goal is to save some lives, or just bring comfort to women by calming their fears.

On The Lighter Side

I gained inspiration for my first humor book, *Hormones From Hell*, when I was in my gynecologist's office, lying on a steel examination table with my legs hoisted up in different time zones, shivering in my 2-inch by 2-inch examination gown, in a room whose temperature hovered around 30°F.

SURVIVING AN EMPTY NEST
WITH THE BOUNCE PLAN

Your Spiritual Fulfillment

Often, it doesn't matter whether we are stay-at-home moms or have careers. We may still feel spiritually empty and unfulfilled. If you are afraid of even thinking about a new life and wonder what you can do to make yourself feel happy, fulfilled, and contributing to society, here's one way. Be a volunteer. What kind? Where? Honestly, it would take me the rest of this book to list areas where one can be a volunteer. But for starters, how about volunteering at a hospital?

When I was married to a doctor, I did hospital volunteer work for more than fifteen years. I baked, sold raffle tickets, worked on fundraisers, took blood pressures, and was the president of the woman's auxiliary for a year. And, you know what? It was a happy and totally fulfilling part of my life. I loved what I was doing.

Every time I walked down the corridor of the children's wing and saw those kids with their little bald heads suffering with cancer, I'd get down on my knees and thank God for my health and the health of my family. It was a huge wake-up call. It changed the way I thought about my life. It really made me think twice about ever complaining again about the lack of anything in my life.

Another fulfilling thing to do is work in a homeless kitchen. When you see people who have to worry about where they are going to sleep that night, or where their next meal is coming from, it shifts your perspective profoundly. Helping the less fortunate will provide you with spiritual fulfillment and purpose. And the best part is that it takes no skills—only compassion.

Your Physical Fulfillment

You will need to keep healthy and strong to take on the busy life that is ahead of you! As we age, we especially need to focus a lot more on our physical bodies. We must start paying closer attention and respecting them more. Have you ever noticed the difference in stamina and appearance of a fifty-year-old who exercises regularly and one who doesn't? I rest my case.

Since exercising is another passion of mine, I have a few suggestions to help get you back into shape. You have the time now, but you'll need to get motivated. Keep affirming that since the time-consuming job of parenting is over, you will be starting a new chapter in your life. Realize you'll need the energy and wellness to make it a great one! Here are my suggestions:

1. Join a gym. Build up your muscular strength, endurance, and stamina with cardiovascular exercise. You will feel great, lose weight, and get into the best shape of your life.
2. If a gym is too intimidating, start by walking around your block. Try walking a little faster and a little longer, every week or so, until after a few months, you are able to jog for half a mile. Keep setting new goals for yourself.
3. When you gain enough stamina and muscle tone to feel more confident, try taking classes in a more challenging workout. Step aerobics, kickboxing, cycling, jazzercize, and resist-a-ball are all excellent cardiovascular workouts. Nowadays, there are gyms that

also offer some rigorous dancing classes in salsa and hip-hop. They are not only fun, but they also really get your heart rate up. You can do any one of these classes. No excuses! Heck, I'm a sixty-year-old grandma, and I do them all!

4. Learn a new sport, such as tennis or golf. The added bonus for these sports is that people often build a whole new set of friends and make a social life with people who share their passion.

Make wellness a top priority in your life. Do whatever it takes to have a robust, healthy, and well-nourished body. It is an integral part of maintaining a happy life. As they say, "Without your health, you have nothing."

Your Emotional Fulfillment

Here are some suggestions for bouncing back from an empty nest into an exciting and rewarding life of *your* choosing:

1. Challenge your mind. Go back to school. Get another degree or finish your old one. Take computer courses. Learn a new language. The sky's the limit.

2. How about using your knowledge and experience from your years of parenting to become a family counselor? Take the necessary courses and get certified. You're a natural.

3. Yearning to broaden your horizons? Take advantage of all of your newfound free time and use it for travel. Through the magic of the Internet, it's possible to be your own travel agent and find great bargains for hotels, airfares, and tours. You can enter a whole new

world that before now was way too expensive. You can be as local or globally ambitious as your search will bring you!

4. Go ahead and write that novel you've had in your head all these years. Use your life experience to create something memorable. It's incredibly therapeutic to get your ideas, emotions, and beliefs down on paper.

5. Do you enjoy keeping the checkbook or doing the yearly taxes? This is no small task. Why not work part-time for a big tax firm or even go back to school and become a CPA? Ditto for becoming a paralegal or an attorney. The point is that there are many levels of many professions you can choose that fit into your time constraints.

6. Use your artistic and creative talents to open a business from your kitchen table. Make clever gift baskets, decorate T-shirts, or design costume jewelry—just to name a few.

7. Spend time with your grandchildren. I find that at sixty years old, I have the time and patience I lacked at twenty-five to sit down with children and really enjoy them. It's a great way to make up for the stuff I still feel guilty about *not* doing with my own kids!

8. Read biographies of successful people. Learn from them, and be inspired by them.

9. Do you love to cook? How about starting a small catering business from your kitchen? Find a niche such as preparing diet meals or catering cocktail parties.

10. Do you love to go and look at other people's homes? Then why not get your Realtor's license? You can stay busy, make money,

and feel really proud of yourself.

These are just a few of literally thousands of options open to you. All you need to do is decide what you really love and then create a career around it. It's as simple as it sounds, too. When you're doing what you love, you won't even feel like you're working. Plus, you're giving yourself a life that has purpose and meaning. And from those seeds springs a happy life.

Conflict:

Emotional

CHAPTER 7

Family Conflict:
And Justice For All

THE PARADOX

Life is full of rules that are not only confusing, but they can be paradoxical, as well. For example, we are told that if you are the kind of personality who is quick to anger and blow up over things, then you're a good candidate for a heart attack or a stroke. Yet, on the other hand, if you repress your anger, you're apt to develop a stress-related disease like an ulcer or colitis. Seems like a no-win situation, doesn't it?

So what are we supposed to do? After all, negative emotions like anger, envy, and hate are all inherent to our human psyche. When we experience them, our brains interpret them as danger and automatically shift us into self-preservation mode, called *fright or flight*. It produces chemicals that raise our blood pressure and increase our adrenaline in an effort to quicken our responses. We are not zombies. It is impossible *not* to feel these emotions when triggered, and it's also not healthy to repress them. Doing so can make the emotion surface in another form, such as panic attacks or depression, or even in a physical manifestation, such as irritable bowel syndrome.

So how do we reconcile this dilemma? We're all human. It's impossible to avoid feeling emotions that will, ultimately, hurt us. But it's up to us to find healthy, socially acceptable outlets for these emotions. That's the only way we'll be able to let go and not become obsessively controlled by them.

Our negative emotions can be expressed actively or passively. Let's say that someone really upsets us. We can respond in one of three ways:

Aggressively: By shouting, throwing things, or physically attacking a person.

Passively: By internalizing our feelings and becoming silent, or even avoiding that person.

Passive-Aggressively: By not acting out directly against the person, but instead reacting with behavior that will somehow affect him or her indirectly.

On The Lighter Side

They say it's better to be married to passive-aggressives because even though they may desperately want to strangle you, they don't do anything about it.

No matter which way we choose to react, holding on to any of these negative emotions will eat away at our insides. Besides anger, there are a lot of other destructive emotions, including:

- Resentment
- Jealousy
- Envy
- Hate
- Insecurity
- Inferiority
- Hopelessness
- Anxiety
- Depression

Any one of these feelings is not easily resolved, either. They are powerful feelings that stem from conflict and often manifest themselves as physical illness or emotional dysfunction.

GOOD MARRIAGES DON'T JUST HAPPEN

Happy marriages take work. That sounds like another paradox, doesn't it? One would think that if two people are so compatible and happy, it wouldn't take any work. But don't kid yourself—it does. During the course of a long marriage, there are going to be plenty of upsets. Some will be small and annoying, and others will be full-blown crises that threaten to rip the marriage apart.

My second marriage, which lasted eighteen years, ended because there were a few core issues that were totally insurmountable. My ex-husband spent our entire marriage abusing alcohol and drugs in an attempt to run away from the terrible secret he was keeping—he was gay. Sadly, there was no resolution for us. The healthy thing was for us to part, with love, and both move on to new lives. Thankfully, we were both able to do this, and today we are good friends. We have both moved on to happier and healthier relationships.

My second marriage is in its fourteenth year. We are happy, compatible, and still very much in love. However, we are not June and Ward Cleaver. Our lives have periods that are far from serene and blissful.

My husband has four daughters from previous marriages, and I have two sons. When you put that many kids, ex-spouses, and other extended family members into the pot, it's bound to generate a lot of steam! Every one of us has brought his own baggage into the mix. Add the fact that Mark is Jewish and I am Catholic, and it's a wonder we don't keep a counselor on speed dial!

On The Lighter Side

When I married a Jewish man and moved to the West Coast, my friends were concerned about how I was going to handle the problem of how I would celebrate our different religious holidays. After a while, I really got irritated from hearing the same thing over and over. So when someone would ask if I was still planning on celebrating Christmas in Connecticut, I'd give them my curt reply, "From now on, I'll be celebrating Hanukkah in Santa Monica!"

Our problems are pretty typical of a divorced couple with blended families. However, we have always managed to work through them, let go of our anger, and get back to a happy life. How are we able to do this? Well, I, for one, try as hard as possible to practice what I preach. And, trust me, it isn't always easy. There were occasions when I forgot to take my own advice, too. A couple of times, when we were going through particularly tough upsets, I actually stayed in bed all day. One time, I even stayed in a nearby hotel for a night to temporarily escape to a calmer place.

A FAMILY IN CRISIS

I'm going to tell you about the biggest crisis of my married life and share how I was able to successfully deal with it. And, believe me, it was a *huge* problem. But we managed to resolve it successfully by working the six principles of the Bounce plan.

This is what happened.

The Beginning

When I was recovering from cancer and bilateral mastectomy surgery, it took every bit of my time and concentration to put myself back on the path to wellness. I had more than just physical healing to accomplish. During a few years prior to my cancer diagnosis, Mark and I were experiencing the usual power struggles and turmoil common to any couple in a new marriage. We had our share of arguments, and we butted heads more than once. All of this conflict had left me with residual feelings of resentment. So, I had a lot of work in store to heal myself on an emotional level. I also needed to work on healing myself spiritually and come to terms with my disease and my mortality.

It was during this time that the biggest crisis of my marriage happened. Talk about bad timing! My husband's ex-wife had experienced a major slip in her twelve years of sobriety. Actually, it had been a series of slips, apparently going on for more than a year. My husband and his older daughters were understandably concerned about the welfare of his youngest daughter. She was thirteen years old, living with her mother and stepfather, and being negatively impacted by her mother's problems. As a result, she was doing poorly in school, acting out in negative ways, and not telling the truth. In general, she was heading down a very self-destructive path.

Mark's older daughters lived in different states. However, both of them called to voice their concerns about their half-sister's welfare. They felt strongly that their sister should be taken from her mother's home and live with Mark and me until she turned eighteen.

Passing judgment about the feelings and opinions of all the parties concerned, in terms of being right or wrong, is not my focus here. Obviously, everyone was passionate about his own opinion and convinced he had the right one.

My Point Of View

I knew there was absolutely no way I could commit to a three-year or more span of becoming a full-time parent to a troubled teenager. I was fifty-four years old and fighting the battle of my life recovering from cancer. At that time, I did not have the extra energy or emotional equanimity necessary to take on such an enormous responsibility. I felt like I could not do a successful job for my step-daughter. I believed that taking on a troubled teenager would put so much stress on me I might be more apt to suffer a recurrence, or at least, prolong my healing process. I felt that there were other options available to help my stepdaughter.

His Point of View

Naturally, my husband was adamant that we should raise his daughter. He was, understandably, feeling guilt, fear, and all the other emotions any parent would feel when faced with a crisis like this one. But I was just as adamant in my feelings because I felt like I was *fighting for my life*. As a result, he developed feelings of anger and resentment toward me. We had been married for seven years and weathered our share of difficulties, but this one looked like it was going to tear us apart.

Fast Forward: A Positive Solution

We found a phenomenal boarding school that offered a curriculum specializing in my stepdaughter's passions: music and the performing arts. The school was nearby, located on top of a lovely mountain. During the year she was there, her mother went into a full-time rehab facility and successful recovered. She needed that time to be alone, without parenting responsibilities, in order to devote herself to her healing and recovery. My stepdaughter needed to get out of her unhealthy home environment and go into one that provided structure, rules, and goals—all of the things she wasn't getting at home. The boarding school accomplished that and much more. They set the bar, and she rose to the challenge. Her grades went from D's and F's to A's and B's. Her self-esteem rebounded, and she was the happiest I had seen her in years.

Implementing The Bounce Plan

Let there be no misconception, though. Happiness and serenity did not just magically appear for us. It took more than a year to work through our emotions of anger and resentment and resolve our differences. But we hung in there and did it. We worked the Bounce plan—or rather, it worked us! Here's how we achieved a happy resolution, using the six principles of Bounce:

BE POSITIVE:

We both made a conscious decision to adhere to the positive vision that we would get through all of this. We maintained the attitude that our marriage was *not* falling apart but admitted that this problem was a threat to it. But, no matter how tough it got, we held the positive thought that our love and commitment to each other would see us through to a positive ending.

OVERCOME STRESS:

During this crisis, I went out and bought several books that taught me how to relieve stress through meditating. Every day, without fail, I'd sit in my back yard amongst my beautiful hibiscus and bougainvillea trees and meditate in the sunshine.

When a virtual tornado of emotions surrounds you, you have to reach deep inside to find your core—your eye of the storm, if you will. It is of enormous benefit to help dissipate those strong negative emotions that are wreaking havoc on your body. Emotions of anger and jealously and feelings of isolation must be cleared away in order to allow room for the healing elements of love and hope to enter.

When you are embroiled in turmoil, your subconscious will try to work it out in your dreams. That's why we experience upsetting dreams, or even nightmares. In these dreams, we feel profound sadness, fear, anger, and many of the emotions we're dealing with when we're awake. So, it's very important to go to sleep in the calmest state of mind possible. That's why I got into the habit of meditating at night, too.

UPLIFT YOURSELF:

I also made a conscious effort to avoid well-meaning but negative-thinking friends, who believed the only solution to my crisis was divorce. I made sure that Mark and I hung out only with couples who had happy, loving, and healthy marriages.

I sought advice only from those girlfriends who liked and respected my husband. I avoided discussing my problems with those women who offered nothing but criticism of him. I was interested only in getting constructive advice about how to work through the issues. I am truly a girl's girl. I love and respect my girlfriends and have chosen them because they are positive thinkers from whom I learn a lot.

No matter how upset Mark and I became during our counseling sessions, we made a point of going to our favorite comedy club every weekend. Even if we drove there in stony silence, we always left feeling relaxed. I cannot tell you how therapeutic it was for us to enjoy a laugh together. Never underestimate the healing power of laughter. There are scientific studies supporting the fact that it produces endorphins, which in turn help strengthen the immune system by increasing the number of T-cells. The old adage, "Laughter is the best medicine" isn't just some old wives tale. It's a scientific fact!

NATURAL FOODS:

During the time we were embroiled in our marital problems and my health problems, there was no question that we had to counteract the negative effects of stress with as healthy a diet as possible. Our bodies had been under attack from stress for the last several years. My immune system had already been compromised to the point of disease. So I had to find a way of undoing the damage and build my immune system back to functioning optimally.

As I was recovering, I read a lot about wellness. I was especially interested in the merits of organically grown foods and their positive effect on the body. This is when I took up juicing and began cooking healthy, fresh, balanced meals. No matter how stressed we were, or how much I didn't feel like cooking, I *made myself* do it. Why? Because I knew that this marital crisis would pass. And, no matter what the outcome, neither of us would regain a good quality of life if we were debilitated by stress-related diseases.

Besides, it was a positive action. I showed Mark that I loved him by taking care of his health, too. It was like saying, "Honey, I know we'll get through this—and I want to us to stay healthy." I know he really appreciated my efforts, too.

COUNSELING:

There was no question that this issue was bigger than both of us. It threatened to consume our marriage. We both realized that there was no way we could resolve this issue without going for professional help. This issue was so explosive we couldn't even discuss it for five minutes without getting into a shouting match. So, we found a therapist who specialized in family and couple counseling. And yes, it was both expensive and time consuming. But our marriage and our health were at stake, so we did what we had to do.

On The Lighter Side

I will admit that there was one occasion when the situation became so potentially explosive that in order to avoid a huge confrontation, I not only moved myself into another room, I moved myself into another state! Once, I went to a friend's home in Nevada to chill out for a few days until we were able to talk with each other without going ballistic.

For the first couple of months, we went to sessions three times a week. Mark would attend one alone, then I'd do the same, and then we'd go together. In the beginning, it was very, very difficult. Our nerves were raw, and we were very angry with each other. So, our therapist made us promise not to discuss any of the issues at home. He told us to save them for the sessions and try to maintain a peaceful atmosphere at home. Our home had to be a safe haven for both of us until the storm passed.

Somehow, we were able to do this. However, as soon as we got into the sessions, all hell broke loose. As we began delving into the main issue, lots of other unresolved issues kept popping up. Each of us voiced a lot of discontents we didn't even know the other had been harboring. Talk about cleaning house! During that first month, tensions ran high, and we usually ended up shouting. That's why we needed the objective, independent voice of a therapist to prevail. Otherwise, the discussions would have degenerated into total chaos.

A therapist's role is not unlike a referee's. He makes you listen to the other person without interrupting him. Then, he clarifies any issues that you might be misinterpreting. After we aired our opinions, the therapist offered his thoughts and assessment of the situation. What really worked in our favor was that we both respected and trusted him. So, when he offered an opinion, we always took it to heart and followed his advice.

On The Lighter Side

There were times I actually felt sorry for our referee—I mean, therapist. We were probably one of the biggest challenges of the man's professional career! It wouldn't have surprised me at all if he had come to our sessions wearing a striped shirt and blowing on a whistle.

It took about a year of heavy-duty counseling, but because we invested the time, we came out of it with a much stronger marriage than before. We were able to repair our relationship and arrive at a more stable, understanding, and loving place than we had ever been. But, it wasn't only Mark and I who benefited from the counseling. Thanks to therapy, the rest of our family also moved on to a better life.

EXERCISE:

When I was recovering from breast cancer surgery, I became more committed than ever to my workouts in the gym. I let nothing, but nothing, keeps me from working out six days a week! In my mind and my heart, I will always believe that exercising is the most important thing a person can do to keep his immune system functioning optimally.

It was also the best possible way to work off my feelings of anger, resentment, and frustration when going through this marital crisis. No matter how upset I felt after a particularly confrontational session, the endorphins produced during exercise gave me the quick fix I needed to calm my body and my mind. I have always been convinced that my exercise regimen was a key factor in allowing my body to heal so quickly. But now, I was actually seeing how beneficial it was in helping me *heal from* and *let go* of those destructive emotions.

All six principles of Bounce worked synergistically and allowed us to reach a place of complete healing. We were able to surmount a seemingly insurmountable problem, and actually bounce back to a more tolerant and loving relationship. Will this be the last big, divisive issue for us? Are you kidding? With our convoluted family tree, there's always another angry head of the Hydra popping up. But, so far, we have been successful. Each time we're able to work through a problem, we gain confidence in our ability to tackle anything life throws at us. We're living proof that the Bounce plan really works.

CHAPTER 8

Relationship Struggles: *Friendly Fire*

MANO VS. MANO

Next time you're in a bookstore, check out how many relationship books are on the shelves. It seems like they outnumber all of the other categories two to one. I guess that tells us something, huh? It means that couples of all ages are plagued with problems about getting along, and they're looking for help. Whether those couples are involved romantically or in business situations, or any other kind of union, they all must be experiencing problems.

Is it any wonder? People act according to their own beliefs, opinions, and usually in their own self-interest. It's just human nature. Sure, it would be ideal if we all shared *the same* opinions and beliefs, but *we don't*. Therefore, it's inevitable that conflicts are going to arise.

Some conflict in any relationship is helpful. It means we feel free enough to express our own opinions, even if they differ from the other person's. This is a good thing. But, when the conflicts are occurring too frequently, we need to be concerned. If the fighting goes beyond moderation, it's going to generate substantial negative feelings that will cripple the communication.

Any form of partnership works best when the partners are compatible, whether it's business, platonic, or romantic. A peaceful atmosphere is essential in maintaining a healthy, long-term relationship. Let's face it. A steady diet of conflict is counterproductive. Over time, built-up resentments will eventually destroy the love in any partnership.

FRIENDS AND LOVERS

I'm going to focus this discussion on dating and marriage. However, keep in mind that the principles discussed here can apply to *any* kind of relationship.

Trying to build a happy life with a mate seems to be on everyone's agenda. We're always hoping that some special person will fulfill our lives. But I think that we often get so involved in our own egos that we tend to forget the fundamental purpose of dating. It's like searching for that perfect outfit that's going to make you feel happy and good about yourself. You probably won't settle for the first one you try on. It usually takes "trial and error" before you get the perfect fit.

Dating works the same way. It's a series of trials—and very complicated ones at that. Therefore, if two people are not suited, it should *never* be thought of as a personal failure. Instead of trying to change the other person, one should keep searching until he meets a person compatible enough to sustain a lifetime of happiness together.

If the outfit doesn't fit, we wouldn't go blaming ourselves and fall into a deep depression. It should be the same with dating. One must always remain positive and use his energy to keep searching until he finds the *right fit*.

On The Lighter Side

Apparently, it's no easy task! I can't tell you how many women I meet in my travels who tell me that they could have written the book, *Dates from Hell*.

DO OPPOSITES ATTRACT?

In a word, yes. They often do. However, in my experience, those differences can eventually cause a huge rift from the continued disgruntlement with each other. It's not uncommon for a person to end up being turned off by or even hating the differences that initially drew her to a person.

For the long haul, couples that have more in common are usually happier with each other. Having the same goals and ideals reduces the chances for conflict. And don't forget: the whole purpose of a relationship is to make you happier, not *unhappier*. But a steady diet of conflict will erode your physical and mental health, producing feelings of anxiety, anger, and unhappiness in you.

AREAS OF CONFLICT IN A RELATIONSHIP

- Sex
- Money
- Religion
- Alcohol

- Drugs
- Children
- In-laws
- Fidelity

- Friends
- Careers
- Other family members

The more compatible your thinking in any of these areas, the more peaceful your relationship will be. Most of the issues listed above are those that couples should be able to work out together. Even if it takes counseling, most of the problems with these issues can be resolved.

However, there are a few issues that I believe are so difficult to resolve, they will be the cause of nothing but misery and continual conflict between couples. For your own survival, there comes a time when the wisest thing to do is throw in the towel. I am going to discuss the issue of alcohol addiction because I experienced it firsthand in my second marriage. Also, because drinking is such a common problem in relationships, it needs to be addressed. I have based my opinions not only on my own experience, but also on those I have observed over many years in my friends' lives.

PARTY HEARTY

Most young couples start out their dating experience with lots of partying. Why not? Life should be fun. Young people should take advantage of their freedom before shouldering the responsibilities of marriage and children.

Dating couples spend a lot of time in bars, dancing, drinking, and staying out late. In fact, a great part of their social lives revolves around alcohol. Fun, huh? But after a year or so, usually one of the people in the relationship tires of this existence and decides the drinking *has to stop*. The conflict arises when the other *doesn't*. This particular conflict is so commonplace, it's just staggering. It's not only prevalent in twenty-year-olds but also in many fifty-and sixty-year-olds that are dating or married.

On The Lighter Side

My married girlfriends and I have a pact that if we ever get dumped by our husbands and are forced to frequent bars wearing miniskirts, 5-inch stiletto heels and way too much eye makeup, we are to immediately shoot each other.

Here's the hard fact. You cannot sustain a peaceful, happy dating relationship or a marriage when one person is addicted to alcohol, drugs, sex, or whatever. Being in a relationship with an addicted person will breed unhappiness and problems that are neverending.

The poignant 1962 movie *The Days Of Wine And Roses*, starring Jack Lemmon and Lee Remick, brilliantly depicted this problem. The story was about the conflict that occurs in a relationship when one person gets sober and the other doesn't. Here's the basic truth in real life that the movie so brilliantly brought home: An alcoholic *never* wants the party to stop. So, when faced with the possibility of spending his life with a sober partner, a major conflict erupts. It may take the form of outright, vicious arguments, with innumerable ultimatums issued by the sober participant. Or it may follow the more manipulative road of the alcoholic spouse's constant attempt to *romance* the sober partner into drinking again. These relationships can function—albeit, function on an unhealthy level—only if *both* spouses are drinking.

Therefore, it becomes the sober spouse's decision whether he wants to remain and try to work it out or leave. However, if he does choose to remain, he will have to sacrifice a lot of his energy, time, and stamina just to survive. But it can be done. There are millions of people who join Al-Anon and other groups that can help them navigate their situations. Their goal is to make you start concentrating on your own health and well-being, instead of expending all your energies trying to "fix" the other person.

MY STORY

There are several types of alcoholic personalities. I was married to the *binge drinker* kind of alcoholic. My husband could go for weeks, or even up to a year, without drinking. However, for most of our eighteen-year marriage, he drank heavily on the weekends. His drinking would affect his behavior in ways that included making a fool of himself at social functions, causing depressive or angry episodes, and making unwise business decisions when under the influence. But no matter what form it took, it was always destructive to himself and those around him. His drinking, over time, eroded many personal and professional relationships, not to mention our marriage.

Another problem common to alcoholics is that even when they aren't drinking, they still have the problem of their addictive behavior manifesting itself in other ways. During the brief periods when he wasn't drinking, my husband switched to a dependency on prescription drugs. During these times, he was in many ways even more out of control than he was on alcohol. He would spend money foolishly, and his professional relationships began to deteriorate as he became more and more paranoid as a result of the drugs he was taking.

But no matter how long or short the periods of sobriety, he always returned to drinking. During my eighteen years of marriage, I issued dozens and dozens of ultimatums to him to "quit drinking or else." But, even if I got a temporary respite, when he started drinking again, it always escalated. Why? He was physically and emotionally addicted and never sought treatment.

After fifteen years of frustration and unhappiness, I finally began going to Al-Anon meetings. I was desperate because his drinking had not only eroded our marriage but also was making me sick—emotionally, physically, and spiritually.

Emotionally, I was anxious all the time. Physically, it manifested in fibrocystic breast disease, which flared up when I experienced severe stress during his drinking binges. Even worse, my anxiety was exacerbated by my smoking way too many cigarettes, which I thought were helping calm my nerves. Spiritually, I felt abandoned—like God had forgotten me.

Surviving His Addiction

Basically, Al-Anon is a program that teaches you how to handle the stress of living with an addicted person on a day-to-day level. Its fundamental philosophy is that the spouse of the alcoholic needs to stop using his time and energy trying to make the alcoholic stop drinking. Instead, it shows you how to start channeling those energies into yourself, to make you more productive, healthy, and happy. And, when you achieve this, you're more likely to be willing to remain in the marriage. Al-Anon believes that when the addicted person is no longer nagged or co-depended, he will often seek sobriety on his own. They feel that marriages can be saved when the spouse implements this philosophy.

This program has worked for millions of people. It allows the alcoholic and nonalcoholic spouse to continue in their marriage, avoiding conflicts about the drinking. Al-Anon helped me a lot. However, in the final analysis, I ended up taking a different action than the programs hopes for. I left my marriage.

Self-Preservation

I attended Al-Anon meetings for three years. I followed their program and became more immersed in my writing. I worked out in the gym regularly. I stopped nagging my husband about his drinking. I stopped making excuses for his behavior. I also stopped accompanying him to parties, where I knew he'd get drunk and embarrass us both. I did all of the things they recommended, *except* that I left the marriage.

It was not an overnight decision—it just gradually evolved. After three years of listening to, observing, and contemplating what other Al-Anon members were doing to remain in their relationships, I instinctively knew I did not want to do the same. I was unwilling to base my life on what it took to remain with an alcoholic. I didn't want to attend meetings five times a week, or even once a week, for that matter, in order to deal with my husband's addiction. He was so in denial about his problem, he had never even considered AA. So, I had no guarantee he would ever even *try* to get sober.

Maybe after fifteen stressful years, the love I had initially felt for him had been too seriously compromised for me to remain in the marriage. Looking back, I probably waited too long to seek help from Al-Anon. But whatever the reasons, the bottom line was that I was emotionally drained, physically ill, and spiritually adrift. I knew that in order to save myself (and my children) on all three levels, I had to walk away. Maybe the philosophy of Al-Anon worked *too* well on me. It helped me to get strong enough emotionally, spiritually, and physically to make that decision *for my own survival.*

After we split up, I kept practicing the principles of the program. I ended up writing a bestseller and moving on into a happier life and a healthier marriage. It was also the best thing for my ex-husband, too. As it turned out, his alcoholism was only a symptom of his real issue—he was embroiled in a lifelong struggle of trying to hide his homosexuality. So, now he was finally free to feel comfortable with whom he really was.

A BRIDGE TOO FAR

My point is that, sometimes, two people will never have enough compatibility to sustain a successful relationship. When your core beliefs, ethics, and goals are so different as to never be reconcilable, I believe that it's not only okay to throw in the towel, but *necessary* for your own survival. This action should never be seen as a personal failure. If you stay in a place of blaming yourself, you'll never be able to move ahead to a happier life.

There is no rule that says you must devote your entire life trying to resolve an irresolvable situation. In fact, it's self-destructive. If you make a mistake, recognize it, and move on. The sooner you come to terms with the fact that your situation is too self-destructive to remain, the healthier it is for you. Then you need to move on in a new direction with your life. That's how you become a survivor.

So, how do we move on? Sure, it's a lot easier said than done. But we start by healing all sides of ourselves. The Bounce plan I developed has its origins in the Al-Anon philosophy. The right answers will come to you when you are physically sound, spiritually at peace, and emotionally stable enough to make good decisions, grounded in clear thinking.

BOUNCING BACK: FOR TWO

My ex-husband and I both went on to better things. He finally sought treatment and kicked his alcohol and drug addictions. He also found a wonderful life partner. I went on to a rewarding career as an author and speaker. Had we stayed together, neither of us could have had the chance at these better lives for ourselves.

Of course, we loved each other. But love wasn't enough to bridge that kind of a gap between us. We spent most of our married life wasting all our productive energies for cross-purposes:

• I was constantly trying to get him to *quit drinking*.
• He was manipulating me and everyone else in his life so he could *keep drinking*.

When I look back, I realize how much energy we expended in trying to get the other to change his point of view. It was a waste of our time and energy trying to resolve an irresolvable conflict. It wasn't until we turned our energies to helping ourselves that we began to heal.

The Lighter Side

When friends want to know how my ex-husband and I managed to stay married for eighteen years under the circumstances, I smile and tell them it was easy. We followed the Clinton policy: "Don't ask, don't tell." If we hadn't, we'd be living in the Bush era of "shock and awe."

HOW TO BE A SURVIVOR

I have come to realize that even back then, I was working on the beginnings of my Bounce plan. I exercised, thought positive thoughts, ate a healthy diet, and sought counseling. They were instinctive actions for self-preservation.

This is why it's so important to practice the principles of the Bounce plan in your everyday lives. If you are searching for a wonderful relationship, the Bounce plan will put you in a strong and healthy position to choose the right person—and not out of emotional need. When you choose out of insecurity, you're more likely to settle for all kinds of unacceptable behaviors in that person. Be aware of that big, looming red flag, if you're trying to forge a relationship with an addicted person. It's really easy for the "healthy" person to become self-destructive in an attempt to escape the pain and helplessness he's bound to feel. Lifetime decisions based on insecurity and neediness are usually disastrous ones. Wise choices are made when a person is emotionally clear, physically strong, and spiritually at peace.

Use the Bounce plan to get yourself in the best shape possible when searching for compatibility. And, if you're already in a relationship riddled with problems, use it to get strong enough to make the right decision about whether to stay. If you're already in a happy relationship, God bless! However, you should never cease striving to strengthen every side of yourself to improve your quality of life and gain further happiness.

Remember: Nobody can *make* you happy. Only you can do that. But a happy, fulfilled person can bring a lot to a relationship that will help keep it working well. When you have the skills to turn the bad times into potentially good ones, your life will become more meaningful, productive, and healthier—all leading to greater personal happiness.

CHAPTER 9

Inner Conflict:
At War With Yourself

THE HIGH COST OF CONFLICT

As human beings, we can be *conflicted* over any number of issues, such as money, relationships, or certain beliefs. But, one thing is for sure. Prolonged conflict will take its toll on us in one way or another. It can cause physical problems, from nervous tics to any number of diseases in any organ of our bodies. Emotionally, it can be the root of depression, aggressive behavior, or anxiety. Spiritually, it puts us at odds with the universe, plaguing us with questions for which we have no answers. It disconnects us from other people and sets us spiritually adrift.

Our parents are responsible for teaching us a set of moral values to live by. Once we have internalized these standards, they will influence our behavior for the rest of our lives. We, in turn, will teach them to our children, and they to theirs. These values are passed on for generations and are collectively called *ethics*. When we accept and practice these ethics, they become a part of our *conscience*.

The basic difference between an emotionally sound person and a sociopath is that the latter has no conscience. He has no internalized set of rules by which he governs his actions. He works from narcissistic impulses, in contrast to the rest of us, whose conscience helps determine our actions.

Living with a conscience is not always easy. There are times we want to do something that our conscience says is wrong. And, if we go against our conscience and do it anyway, our actions will produce an inner conflict.

'TIL DEATH DO US PART

I'd like to focus specifically on the inner conflict produced when one decides to leave a marriage, since we talked about walking away from relationships with irresolvable conflicts in the previous chapter. Because divorce touches us all in some way, we can benefit from learning how to handle the resulting inner conflicts it produces.

From an early age, we are taught to honor the institution of marriage. We place a huge premium on marriage and family. It's held sacred in our culture and even considered a sacrament in some churches. Therefore, when we take the vow, "for better or worse. . .'til death do us part," we're determined to uphold it. To show our commitment, we take this vow in front of our families, our friends, and God. It's an awesome promise, and one that will lead to many heavy consequences if broken.

All this being said, many people find that after a few years, they're miserable in their marriages. They become obsessed with whether or not they should leave. It goes without saying that breaking up a marriage and family has serious consequences for everyone involved. The price is paid not only in terms of money but emotionally and physically as well. Every day, people struggle with the question: "Should I remain in an unhappy marriage forever, or do I leave and possibly destroy the lives of my spouse and kids?"

This profound inner conflict is an extremely common one. All over the country, more people than you can imagine are living out this scenario. Unfortunately, there is no upside to unresolved inner conflict. It wreaks havoc in us on all three levels: physically, emotionally, and spiritually. And if left unresolved, it will eventually harm the individual in some of the following ways:

MANIFESTATIONS OF INNER CONFLICT

Physical/ Emotional
- Ulcers
- Irritable bowel
  syndrome
- Headaches

- Heart problems
- Addictions
- Obesity
- Weight loss

- Back pain
- Alcoholism

Spiritual

- Inability to love
- Abandonment
  of religion

- Inability to find
  peace
- Anger at God

It is not my intention to discuss whether a person should leave a relationship or not. Each case is different and needs to be resolved by the people in it. What I want to stress is that inner conflict cannot rage on, indefinitely, without causing serious side effects. It will take you down. Inner conflict must be addressed just as a physical problem would be. It needs to be healed.

CONSEQUENCES OF DELAY

In the case of my marriage, my ex-husband's inner conflict arose when he tried to hide his sexual persuasion by living his life as a lie. I can only imagine how his inner conflict must have reached a point where it became totally unbearable. That's why he chose to seek relief in alcohol and prescription drugs. He did this for more than thirty years. So over time, he not only ruined his physical health but also became an emotional train wreck from the added problems of his addictions.

It wasn't until we got divorced that he finally faced his issues and was able to resolve them. After he did this, he moved on into a much happier existence, where he was comfortable living in his own skin.

Looking back, I was, unfortunately, a co-dependent in the marriage. My refusal to deal with the issues only prolonged the inevitable. It wasn't until I sought help for myself in Al-Anon that I was able to gain the strength to face the issues honestly.

The really sad part of the story is that now my ex-husband is physically paying the price for his years of addiction to alcohol, tobacco, and drugs. He developed severe emphysema, and he will need a lung transplant to remain alive. He is only sixty-four years old.

I am relating this to you because I really want you to grasp the severity of the consequences of unresolved conflict, whether it is about marriage, friendships, or parental relationships. Unresolved conflict may often lead to destructive behaviors that have a lasting effect on your life, or in some cases, even claim it. That's why it's so critical to incorporate the Bounce plan into your life, so that you will have the tools to work through any conflict to resolution.

FORGIVING HEALS

Whatever your decision, you'll need to take the following steps in order to move ahead:

• Forgive yourself
• Forgive others
• Stop the regrets

There is an old adage that says you can't move ahead until you close the previous chapters of your life. There's a lot of wisdom in that saying. All of your energies must be focused on moving ahead. Whether you remain in the marriage or go it alone, you'll need to make peace with the past by forgiving.

Although my ex-husband and I moved on to better lives, it didn't happen instantly. We both had to work through our lingering anger and resentment toward each other. Eventually, we did it. And, because we have forgiven each other, today our sons' lives are peaceful and without conflict. With the help of meditation and prayer, I have come to accept his choices and have stopped blaming him.

Because I set this example for my sons, they have been able to move forward without hatred or resentment toward their father. They, in turn, have taught me a lot about the power of love and acceptance by their own examples. This is exactly why we are all leading loving and productive lives, free of turmoil and anger. Our lives are working because we are not wasting our energies on negative thoughts and feelings.

IN THE SUNSHINE

I am totally unwilling to waste one precious second of my life on negativity, especially after my experience with cancer. I have worked hard to heal my body, my mind, and my soul. And when all of these elements are in harmony, you can't help but lead a joyous life.

CHAPTER 10

Positive Thoughts:
Positively Create Reality

COME ON, GET HAPPY

When I was in my early twenties, a girlfriend and I were discussing what kind of people we were. She made a statement that had such an impact on me, I still remember her words to this day. She said very matter-of-factly:

"Oh, I'm one of those people who is always happy. . .unless something specific happens that makes me unhappy."

It made me wonder, "Are some people just *born* happy, or do we have to *learn* how to be happy?"

On The Lighter Side

I know that last statement makes me sound like Sarah Jessica Parker narrating a *Sex and the City* scene. The great irony of that show was that even though those women were having more sex than any of us could handle, it didn't seem to improve their dispositions at all.

The truth is that back then I didn't know the answer. I never gave it much thought. But now, I have come to believe that we *are* born happy. Children possess an innately happy spirit; however, for many, it gets repressed during their lives for various reasons.

I always remembered what my girlfriend said about being happy, because she was describing *me*. Basically, I am a happy, positive person who chooses to see everything as the "glass half full." I cannot imagine living a life that is sorrowful or negative. In fact, it scares me. So, when something happens that does make me sad or disappointed, I work hard at learning my lessons from it, move on, and return to my happy frame of mind as soon as possible.

However, I am aware that many people don't operate this way. There are negative thinkers who envy those of us with sunny dispositions. We have all heard snide remarks such as, "She's sooo perky" or, "Who does she think she is—Rebecca of Sunnybrook Farm?"

So, is it possible for those people who are negative in their attitudes to become happier by learning to live in the positive? The answer is yes. But, it takes a shift in their thinking. First, they have to *choose* to be happy. Then, they need to begin *visualizing* themselves this way.

Another reason I always seek the positive in life is that as a cancer survivor, I have learned that thinking positively is crucial in maintaining a life of wellness. This is not a new concept, either. There have been many books written about positive thinking and the power it has in making a person's life happy, healthy, and successful. Remember Dr. Norman Vincent Peale's *The Power Of Positive Thinking?* It was published back in 1952. There is also a series of Dale Carnegie books about positive thinking that have been selling steadily for years. *How To Win Friends and Influence People* was published in 1936 and *How To Stop Worrying and Start Living* in 1944.

THE NATURE OF THOUGHT: WILL SCIENCE AND SPIRITUALITY MERGE?

In this new millennium, it seems like we are re-examining the power of thought on a much more extensive scale. For thousands of years, spiritual teachers have believed that our thoughts are made up of vibrating energy. And they also believed that positive thoughts held a higher vibrational energy than negative ones. Now, traditional science is beginning to enter this arena, and its latest theories are coming closer to what the philosophers have always maintained.

New theories from theoretical physicists about the vibrating properties of subatomic particles are beginning to unravel the mysteries of what thoughts are. As theoretical physics is venturing into new territories like nano-technology and discovering new things about the nature of subatomic particles, the physical sciences are getting closer to the teachings of great spiritual thinkers like Buddha, Pantangeli, and Gandhi.

For example, it has long been a tenet of spiritual teachers that the energy of positive thoughts emanating from a spiritual level can be manifested into reality on a physical level. And now, the newest technological advances are allowing scientists to make discoveries about the possibility of energy transcending known boundaries into unknown dimensions. New knowledge about the nature of energy is approaching the long-held spiritual beliefs about the soul, the nature of creation, and the possibility of parallel dimensions.

THE REAL WORLD: POSITIVE VS. NEGATIVE ENERGY

We seem to be living in a huge paradox. On one hand, we appear to be progressing into an age of spiritual enlightenment, but on the other, it is diametrically opposed to many ongoing negative events on the planet. There are still profound conflicts among people everywhere, an abundance of crime, and unhealthy thinking taking place. Therefore, as we watch the nightly news, we all ask ourselves the same question: "Is it possible to maintain a positive, happy frame of mind with all of these real threats and negativity bombarding us?"

Let me assure you, it is possible. But it must be done on a conscious level. We must make the choice for positive thoughts and images to fill our minds, and likewise, perform positive actions in our lives. Remember, everything originates as thought. Taking it a step further, if we all individually make the conscious effort to live in the positive, then at some period in time there will be enough individuals on this path to make it global. Our collective positive thoughts manifesting themselves in the physical realm will improve life for everyone on this planet.

LIFE IS A BLESSING

Let's take this concept back to a simpler level and apply it to our daily lives. What drives certain people to make the choice to think positive thoughts? I believe it is because these people are really grateful for their lives. In order to live a happy life, the most basic requirement is that you must be truly grateful for it. As a cancer patient who got my life and my health back, I live in a perpetual state of gratitude for my life. I believe that positive thinking and positive actions stem from this premise:

Never take your life for granted. When you live in a state of gratitude, you will not only seek out the positive, but the positive also will seek you out.

Do you want to know the quickest way to become grateful for your life? Visit an ICU unit in a hospital. When you see the courage and the struggle it takes for those patients to hold on to their lives in spite of their suffering, it will change you. You will feel a renewed gratitude for your own life.

KEEP THINKING THOSE GOOD THOUGHTS

We have all heard the phrase "the power of positive thinking." Well, there is actual scientific evidence to back it up. The energy from positive thoughts impacts a person on three levels:

Physical:

Positive thoughts boost the functioning of the immune system by prompting the brain to release neuro-chemicals such as endorphins, serotonin, and dopamine. These chemicals bolster the immune system by actually increasing the production of specific disease-fighting white blood cells.

Emotional:

Certain neuro-chemicals produced by the brain, such as dopamine-act as natural mood elevators. They help lift depression and promote enthusiasm and interest in life. Positive thoughts are also highly motivating forces that keep us succeeding in life. They help the brain to think more clearly, and that in turn allows us to make the constructive actions that ultimately bring about happiness.

Spiritual:

From time immemorial, there have been great spiritual leaders and mystics who used meditation and prayer to manifest positive thoughts into the physical world. They believe that positive thoughts carry a higher vibrational energy that is a healing energy. And, love carries the highest vibrational energy of all. Thus, the energy of love has the potential to heal the body, the mind, and the spirit.

YOU ATTRACT WHAT YOU GIVE OUT

People who are friendly with sunny dispositions naturally attract other people. They also bring out the goodness in others. Hasn't it always been true that the boys and girls in high school who were voted "most popular" were always the friendly kids who weren't "stuck up" and fun to be around?

Well, here's the wonderful thing about positive dispositions: When you give out positive energy in the form of good will and love, you'll attract more of the same back into your life. However, those who project feelings of superiority get resentment and hostility back. But when you project warmth and good will to others, a majority of the time, people will respond to you the same way. That's why positive people *do* have lives that flow more easily and are more successful. However, they do not achieve their happy lives by mere chance. They *make* it happen with their determination to live their lives this way.

Doesn't this make sense? So, why isn't everyone living like this? Well, I know there are people who desperately want to live positive lives but have *no* idea where to begin. So, here are some helpful suggestions for getting your mind to stay focused on the path of living the rest of your life as a positive person.

HOW TO LIVE IN A POSITIVE FRAME OF MIND

1. Change Your Concept Of Failure

If something doesn't work out for you, *stop* believing that you *failed*. Instead, change your thinking. Start thinking of failure as an opportunity to learn from what went wrong. Then, the next time a challenge arises you will welcome the opportunity to use new tactics. You won't get stuck like the rat who repeatedly goes through the same maze that has no cheese at the end.

Once you change your concept of failure into an opportunity to grow and learn, you won't brand yourself a failure. You'll keep your self-esteem intact, and you won't be afraid to move ahead and try again. The disappointments won't cripple you. Instead, you'll learn from them and apply that knowledge to succeed in new, creative ways.

2. Surround Yourself With Other Positive Thinkers

Fill your life with only positive thinkers and people who really care about your welfare and the welfare of others. This doesn't mean that you have to confront or be negatively obsessed about those people who have not lived up to this standard. You cannot change them. Anyway, it's not your job. Instead, release these people with love. You will find that when you live in the company of positive people, your mood and your outlook will brighten from the positive energy surrounding and infiltrating you.

On The Lighter Side

I got rid of those energy-sucking vampires. You know—the one's you don't dare ask the question, "How are you?" because you're stuck there for the next three hours? My life has been so much more peaceful since I got rid of the Debbie Downers!

3. Be Grateful For Your Life

Suppose you had only one year to live. Think about how you would feel and what your actions would be. Then live your life this way. Death is not the real tragedy. Rather, it's looking back on your life and regretting all the happiness, kindness, and fulfilled moments you missed because you didn't recognize and treasure what you had.

The Lighter Side

One of my favorite comics says this: If I only had one year to live, I'd spend it with my ex, because every day with her is like a stinkin' eternity.

Also, learn to be grateful for what you have. Stop being jealous of what others have. Instead, focus on being happy for their successes. When you wish others success and happiness, you will attract it into your own life.

4. Focus on Eliminating Worry In Your Life

The best to way eliminate worry is by concentrating on living in the moment. Work at focusing on and enjoying what you are doing and seeing *right now*. Concentrate on preventing your mind from drifting forward with worry about what *could* happen, or backwards with negative regrets. This wastes the precious moments of now. Also, be grateful for what *you have*. Push away any thoughts that you could be doing something better or that what you have isn't good enough.

Living in the now means living with appreciation and gratitude for every small thing in life—a warm sunny day, the incomparable beauty of nature, the joy that friends and family bring, and countless other blessings.

5. Let Go of the Past

Keep reminding yourself that the past is *over and done*. It exists only in thought. Negative emotions such as regret, guilt, and remorse rob you of your ability to experience the joy of *now*. Past negative experiences should be used only as tools to build a better life in the present.

6. Always Work Toward the Goal of Forgiveness

It is imperative to staying in a positive frame of mind that you not only forgive others but forgive yourself as well. Don't get me wrong.

This is no small task. It's one of the hardest things we can do. But, not forgiving and holding on to resentments depresses the immune system, allowing disease to develop in the body. It also cripples your ability to love. Negative feelings will block love from entering your heart, mind, and spirit. Remember, love is the most powerful healing force available to us.

So, even if you can't forgive one hundred percent, keep working *toward the goal* of loving your enemy. The way to achieve it is through prayer and meditation.

7. Lighten Up

Life should be joyous. Make a conscious effort to seek out humor in all situations and learn to make laughter an integral part of your life. Much of the time, it's our egos that get in the way of enjoying life. The ego keeps us in unforgiving and restricted places. So work on setting your ego aside and stop taking yourself so seriously. Self-importance cripples spiritual growth.

Start right now by making it a priority to lighten up. Instead of watching a depressing or violent movie for entertainment, go to a comedy club. I guarantee you will actually *feel lighter* from using those belly muscles to laugh. Physically, laughter does great things to keep your body healthy. It produces endorphins that actually relax the walls of blood vessels, lowering the blood pressure. Trust me on this. When you start making conscious choices for happiness in all areas of your life, you will feel yourself loosening up and metamorphosizing into a happy person.

8. Give More to Life

Doing positive acts for others takes the focus off of ourselves. People who spend a good deal of their lives giving to others are the happiest and most fulfilled people of all. I'm not talking about just giving material things, either. Give of yourself—your time, your kindness, your humor, and your knowledge. These are the most valuable gifts of all.

One way to make a profound impact on your life is by becoming a volunteer. You can volunteer at any number of places, from old folks' homes to animal shelters. When you give, you will get it back a hundredfold from the universe in terms of love, happiness, and fulfillment. It makes you so much more appreciative of your own life. As I have stated before, when you truly appreciate every day of your life, those days will be filled with happiness.

9. Set Goals for Yourself

These goals can range from the simple, daily goals of accomplishing a task to more lofty, lifetime goals. The point is to stop being idle and wasting time. Focus on your goals and visualize what you want. Then, visualize yourself succeeding at what you desire. Remember, it is a rule of the universe that *you can manifest your thoughts* into reality through meditation.

Those who set goals—daily, monthly, and yearly—get a tremendous sense of pride and fulfillment when they accomplish them. Idle time usually leads to negativity. Aren't we always preaching this to our kids? We work hard at keeping their lives filled with activities that keep them busy. Why? Because we know it will make them happier and keep them away from negative situations. Well, here's a news flash. It isn't any different for adults.

10. Work At Taming Your Ego

When you are able to sublimate your ego, your real spiritual purpose will become clear. Remember, the *real you* is your spirit. *You are not*:

- Your possessions
- Your money
- Your physical body
- Your career

Do not let these things define you, because they are fleeting. If you should lose any one of them, you will be devastated. Also, when you live in a world where you value only material things, you'll constantly feel envious of everyone else. There is always going to be somebody who is better looking, makes more money, or lives in a nicer house. Envy is a negative emotion that eats away at your body and soul, and brings you nothing but unhappiness.

When you truly embrace the concept that your ego is not who you are, you'll be able to lighten up and find your true spiritual self. Then, joy and happiness will come to you.

To Sum Up:

God gave us the power to think and the free will to make choices in our lives. We have a lot more control over our thoughts than we might believe. Making the choice for positive thoughts and actions will allow us to become much happier people.

Leading a positive life impacts us on three levels: physical, emotional, and spiritual. Positive thinking will manifest into good health, happiness, success, and spiritual fulfillment. Make it a top priority to put these ten suggestions into practice right now to help you to begin living a positive and happy life. Don't put it off. As soon as you begin *thinking* you can have a wonderful life, you *will* make it happen!

Part II: THE ACTIONS

CHAPTER 11

Don't Diet: *Eat Healthy*

NATURE HEALS

Everything our bodies require to stay healthy and heal themselves is found on our earth. I think of foods as medicine. For example, if my stomach is upset, instead of taking an anti-acid pill, I'll drink a cup of ginger tea. Since my cancer experience, learning about wellness and nutrition has given me the knowledge that has taken me in this direction.

Natural foods are the way to go. They are the best fuel and the best medicine we can put into our bodies. Nature has provided a planet full of all sorts of healing foods that support every cell in our bodies.

DON'T MESS WITH PERFECTION

The foods that grow naturally are called *whole foods* because all of their parts are intact. And it's the *whole* part that contains all the goodness: the natural vitamins and nutrients that support health.

Unfortunately, we have not learned to leave well enough alone.

Man has developed manufacturing processes that remove many of the parts of the food that contain nutrients. Go figure! For example, grains that grow in nature have their bran and germ intact. But when refined, only the non-nutritious, starchy part remains. This process is done with far too many of our foods. So we need to identify the whole foods from the refined and processed ones.

Whole foods supply all of the right proportions of nutrients. Therefore, stripping and chopping away parts of them is entirely counterproductive. We need to trust that Mother Nature has done her best. Leave her alone, and let her nourish us without interference.

On The Lighter Side

My theory about Ho-Hos and Twinkies is that they bypass the stomach and are deposited directly on the hips.

WHOLE FOODS FOR WELLNESS

When shopping for foods, you should make it a point to look for whole foods. Also, try to buy foods that are labeled "organically grown." This means that they do not contain chemicals, hormones, or pesticides, which are all toxins and can do much damage to our cells.

Try to eat produce that is locally grown because it has a higher nutritional content. It's more likely not to have been treated with preservatives or coated with wax.

VARIETY FOR VIGOR

Even though it's our tendency to eat the same diet of our favorite foods, make an effort to change this pattern. The more varied the foods you eat, the more nutrients you're getting. Remember, each vitamin performs a different supportive function in the body. So, we must ingest a wide variety to cover our nutritional needs.

ORGANIC FOODS: THE ONLY WAY TO GO

I choose organic fruits and veggies because they're grown without pesticides, herbicides, or chemical fertilizers. They also don't contain artificial coloring or wax to make them look better. Personally, I avoid any chicken or beef that has been given hormones to make it plumper. Many cancers are estrogen-dependent, meaning they grow in the presence of hormones. I will occasionally eat free-range chicken from organically raised birds that have not been given hormones.

The Environmental Working Group lists the most contaminated nonorganic foods as:

- strawberries
- spinach
- apples
- peaches
- green beans
- apricots
- cucumbers
- grapes from Chile
- U.S.-grown cherries
- green and red bell peppers
- Mexican-grown cantaloupe

Memorize this list, and make a habit of buying only organically grown varieties of these foods.

ALL FOR ANTIOXIDANTS

Nowadays, it seems like all we ever hear about is antioxidants. What are they, anyway? Okay, let me state this simply: They are vitamins that stop the actions of *free radicals,* which are molecules that damage cell walls and tissues. Free radicals are the culprits of aging, too.

Where do free radicals come from? Actually, our own bodies produce some. But other sources are cigarette smoke, air pollutants, radiation, and pesticides.

The four primary antioxidants are:

- Beta carotene
- Vitamin C
- Vitamin E
- Selenium

Whole Foods That Provide Antioxidants

Beta Carotene: Yellow and orange vegetables and fruits such as: carrots, butternut squash, acorn squash, pumpkin, cantaloupes, apricots, mango, kale, red pepper, and spinach.

Vitamin C: Citrus fruits, strawberries, broccoli, tomatoes, and Brussels sprouts.

Vitamin E: Nuts: hazel nuts, Brazil nuts, almonds, and flaxseed. Fish: shrimp, haddock, salmon, mackerel, and herring.

Selenium: Fish: shellfish, salmon, flounder, sole, perch. Meat: beef, lamb, pork, and liver. Vegetables: cauliflower, green beans, and seaweed.

Grains: Bran, rice, bulgur, and whole wheat.

To Sum Up:

Our bodies require a whole range of vitamins and minerals. The best way to get them is by eating a variety of fruits and vegetables.

SEAFOOD: A SMART SELECTION

Seafood is a perfect food. It's low in fat and high in protein. A variety of seafood will provide a range of the B vitamins, vitamin A, vitamin D, vitamin E, and omega 3 fatty acids.

I am really into shellfish, too. My favorites, shrimp and scallops, contain selenium, the antioxidant that doctors recommend for people who have had cancer. Shellfish are also low in fat and high in omega 3 fatty acids—another recently touted name. What are they?

Omega 3 Fatty Acids:

These are fats found in our nervous systems, our brain, eyes, adrenal glands, and sex glands. They carry oxygen and remove cholesterol from our arteries. They also prevent blood clots, decrease blood pressure, and are anti-inflammatory agents. Omega 3 fatty acids have been associated with a decrease in the incidence of cancer.

Omega 3's are more abundant in fattier fish, such as salmon, sardines, tuna, mackerel, and anchovies. These fish live in colder waters and need the extra fat to retain body heat.

On The Lighter Side

Omega 3's also keep your skin looking young. Susan Lucci from *All My Children* says she eats sardines to get the Omega 3 benefits. Hey, if I could look that good after surviving multiple marriages, kidnappings, near-death experiences, and evil twins, I'd buy the cannery!

A FEW GOOD GRAINS

Grains are the seeds of grasses. Whole grains are especially healthy because they contain healthy fats, vitamins and minerals, besides starch. Their health benefits are well documented and date back to before the Bible. Bran, oatmeal, barley, couscous, spelt, and millet are just a few of the many grains growing on the earth.

Make sure you buy grains that are labeled "whole grain" because the nutritional part hasn't been stripped away. Only whole grains are complex carbohydrates with all of their original parts.

A FEW FOOD FACTOIDS

Cauliflower: The Institute of Food Research in London reports that cauliflower contains an anti-cancer ingredient, AITC, which disrupts cancer cell proliferation. It recommends having two servings weekly to gain this benefit.

Tomatoes: One German study suggests that a daily dose of cooked tomatoes can quadruple your skin's natural sun protection factor (SPF). Tomatoes contain *lycopene*, an antioxidant that prevents free radical damage, which can wrinkle the skin and cause sunspots. Plus, they're rich in phosphorous, a mineral that helps burn body fats and carbohydrates.

Raspberries: These berries are rich in antioxidants that fight free radical damage to the tissues. They also reduce the risk of glaucoma.

Blueberries: According to a USDA study, blueberries contain *anthocyanins* and antioxidants that trigger the growth of neurons in the brain's hippocampus, which controls motor skills, memory, and learning.

Mangoes: This delicious fruit is loaded with the amino acid called *tryptophan*, which triggers the brain to release a chemical called *serotonin*, known to uplift your spirits.

Oranges: Besides the well-known vitamin C boost, the peel of the orange contains the photochemical *limonene*, which helps block abnormal cell growth that can lead to cancer. The peel is dried and powdered into the spice called orange zest. Oranges also contain iron, which helps build the hemoglobin responsible for carrying oxygen to all of our cells.

Sesame seeds: Contain copper that acts as an anti-inflammatory, which lessens joint pain. Warning: The sesame seeds *cannot* be attached to a Big Mac bun!

Eggplant: Contains *protease inhibitors* that stop tumor growth and heal damaged cells.

Shiitake and other mushrooms: Contain zinc that helps the body fight bacteria and viruses.

Organic honey: This is a great substitute for sugar or artificial sweeteners. Honey helps inhibit the growth of *H. pylori*, the bacteria known to cause ulcers and other digestive tract disorders. It also contains a large amount of vitamins, minerals, and antioxidants.

Flaxseed oil: This oil is a wonderful source of omega 3 fatty acids, which help thin the blood and widen the arteries. I use flaxseed oil with balsamic vinegar to make a delicious salad dressing.

Water: Besides just quenching thirst, water provides huge benefits because it doesn't have to be digested or metabolized by the body. Its functions in the body are to:
• help remove waste

- help dissolve substances like mineral salts that maintain the acid/alkaline balance in our body tissues
- transport vitamins and minerals
- help the cells produce energy
- provide lubrication to joints and cushion the eyes and spinal cord

It is true that you should drink at least eight glasses of water a day. To make sure you do, keep the water accessible. I keep bottled water by my bed, in the car, in my gym bag, and just about any place that's easy to reach.

I never drink colas or soft drinks. They contain caffeine, sugars, and phosphorous that deplete minerals and take calcium from your bones. The caffeine makes you anxious and jumpy and exacerbates conditions such as fibrocystic breast disease.

Soft drinks have absolutely no health benefit to them. So, why take up tummy space with something that does nothing for you? I have learned to drink water, juice, or iced tea when I'm thirsty.

To Sum Up:

As a cancer survivor, I have become very aware of nutrition. I look at foods in an entirely different way than I used to. I see foods as medicine and fuel, put on the earth by God, with everything we need to keep our bodies working optimally.

All we have to do is make smart choices by eating a variety of natural, whole foods. For example, choose water instead of carbonated sodas. Buy whole grain bread instead of processed white bread. Eat chicken that has been fed an organic diet and not treated with hormones. Steam a variety of veggies that provide you with all of the essential nutrients. Don't dump three packets of artificial sweetener into a drink when you can use a little organic honey instead.

Besides being better for you, whole foods are honestly more delicious than processed or refined foods. Eating this way will not only increase your wellness, but you'll look a lot younger, too. It is true. When you eat a healthy variety of whole foods, you won't gain weight, your skin will glow, and you'll have a ton of energy.

HOW TO COOK WHOLE FOODS

Steaming:

My favorite way to cook veggies is by steaming them. Steaming preserves the vitamins and minerals a lot better than cooking them in a pot of water. I steam my veggies in the top shelf of my rice cooker. If you don't have one, put the veggies in a steam basket in a pot containing a small amount of water, simmer for about ten minutes and they'll be cooked perfectly.

Many veggies are still good when boiled. However, don't discard the water they're boiled in. Save it for your soups and broths, because it contains the vitamins and nutrients that were boiled out of the vegetables.

Baking and grilling:

Since I eat a lot of fish, sometimes I bake it and other times I grill it. But I never cook it in aluminum foil. Aluminum has been found in the brains of Alzheimer's patients, so I think it best to avoid allowing your food to come into contact with it. This is what I do instead:

Grilling: First, I place the fish in one of those clear oven bags, adding lemon and margarine to it. I twist the tie bag, and then wrap it in foil and place it on the grill. I cook it for about twenty minutes, and voila! The fish poaches in the lemon and margarine in the oven bag, staying moist and retaining all of its vitamins and minerals.

Baking: Sometimes, I coat the fish with a beaten egg and roll it in those delicious Japanese, panko bread crumbs. You can find them in most supermarkets. I place it in a Pyrex oven dish and bake it. Other times, I add seasonings, place the fish on oven parchment paper, and bake it.

Stir frying:

This is an excellent way to cook because it requires only a little bit of oil. The fast frying preserves the nutrients. There is an unlimited combination of foods you can use for stir-fried meals. Besides being nutritious, they're also easy and quick to make. I like to stir-fry different kinds of vegetables with scallops or shrimp. With stir-frying, you can make a delicious, healthy meal in less than ten minutes. Now that's my idea of cooking!

To Sum Up:

Thank goodness our culture is becoming enlightened about healthy diets. We are really becoming aware of how our bad diets are keeping us sick and obese. Nowadays, there are entire sections in bookstores devoted to nutrition. You can't pick up a magazine without reading about healthy foods and great recipes.

So it's time to do your body a big favor and get on the whole food bandwagon. When you make the effort to switch to a healthy, whole food way of eating, it will pay the dividend of continual wellness. Then, if you add a regular exercise regimen, you'll be walking the walk of wellness and vitality.

NOTE: In writing this chapter, I used the book *Healthy Food For Dummies* by Molly Siple, M.S., R.D., published by IDG Books, Worldwide, Inc. for research.

I also got many food facts from various magazines, including *Organic Style*, *First For Women*, and *Good Housekeeping*.

CHAPTER 11

Juicing:
The Power Punch

GET HEALTHY: ASAP

Fruits and vegetables are loaded with vitamins, minerals, and hundreds of other substances that protect against cancer and other diseases. All kinds of medical practitioners are now urging their patients to include more fruits and vegetables in their diets, preferable in raw form or with a minimum of processing. Most guidelines call for five to ten servings of fruits and veggies each day, which is usually just too much food for us to consume. Therefore, juicing is an ideal way to get the recommended servings into our bodies.

When I was recovering from cancer surgery, I focused on rebuilding my immune system and regaining my strength. In order to accomplish this, I knew I had to get as many vitamins and minerals into my body as possible, in a hurry. But I knew there was no way I could eat the tons of food that it would take. So, how was I able to get all those vitamins and minerals in me in a quick, digestible form? I did it with juicing.

JUICING FACTS

- 95 percent of the nutritional content of fruits and vegetables is in their juice.
- Fresh fruits and vegetables are an easy-to-prepare source of vitamins and minerals.
- Juices are absorbed rapidly into the blood stream.
- Juicing is the fastest way your body can digest nutrients.

Freshly prepared juice contains living enzymes, which are proteins that help chemical reactions take place in the body. They are present in raw foods, including fruit and vegetable juices. Eating foods with enzymes aids in digestion. The only thing juicing does not supply is the fiber that is contained in the whole food.

JUICE THE POSSIBILITIES!

When you make your own juices, you have total control over what goes into them. Freshly extracted juices should be consumed right after making them to avoid the loss of vitamin content.

For Best Results:
1. Always wash your fruits and vegetables before juicing them.
2. Try to use only fresh, organically grown produce.
3. If fresh produce is impossible to find, you may use frozen, but make sure it's organically grown.

4. Seasonal fruits may be cut into cubes or slices and frozen, single layer, on a tray. Then place them in freezer bags for storage.

Most of the juicers on the market are pretty good. They all come with easy-to-follow directions about how to use and clean them. They also provide you with basic recipes for making smoothies, vegetable drinks, soups, and other nutritious meals.

JUICE IT UP!

The upside of juicing is that you can get really creative. You are not a slave to a recipe book. Just think about what veggies or fruit combinations taste great together, and experiment. Hey, it's not rocket science. It's just fun! You'll be amazed at how fantastic the flavors of the blended concoctions taste. And the best part is, they not only taste great, but also they're so healthy for you.

Now, for those unadventurous souls out there, I'll give you a few complete recipes (with measurement amounts).

FRUIT SMOOTHIES

Peach Perfection

1 peach

½ cup nonfat vanilla yogurt

1 cup sliced strawberries

5 ice cubes

1 banana

1 packet Stevia sweetener

Nutritional Information: *Calories 115, fat 1g, carbohydrates 22 grams, protein 5 grams, cholesterol 5 milligrams*

. . . .

High Energy Fruit Fizz

1 cup strawberries

1 cup peaches

1 banana

1 cup nonfat yogurt

1 orange (peeled)

1 cup ice cubes

1 cup club soda

Nutritional information: *Calories 173, fat .4 grams, protein 3.7 grams, vitamin A 4 percent, calcium 10 percent, vitamin C 80 percent*

Here are some of my original favorites:

The Marvelous Melon
Three ounces cubes of:

1 cup cubed Honeydew

1 cup of cubed cantaloupe

1 block of tofu

1 cup vanilla yogurt

5 ice cubes

. . . .

Sassy Citrus

1 cup cubed pineapple

1 orange, peeled and sectioned

1 tangerine, peeled and sectioned

1 banana

2 teaspoons honey

3 ice cubes

Okay, now that you've got the basic recipes down, go ahead and wing it! The list on the next page shows some of the wonderful fruits that make the best combinations for smoothies and juice drinks. You may want to juice just one of your favorite fruits, or combine two or more together. Then just add whatever else you desire—protein powder, soymilk, ice cubes, or yogurt, and voila! You've got smoothie!

Blackberries/ Bananas

Strawberries/ Peaches

Blueberries/ Mango

Pineapple/ Oranges

Delicious Smoothie Combos

Make your own personalized drinks by juicing any proportions of the following fruit combos. They'll make fabulous tasting smoothies that are jam-packed with nutrients. If you love strawberries, then add more of them. The beauty of juicing is that there are no rules. So, go ahead. Knock yourself out!

TIPS:

Fizzy: To make juice coolers, just add sparkling water and ice to your finished fruit juice.

Power max: When mixing up your smoothie, add powdered protein instead of yogurt.

Hate milk? Substitute soymilk or tofu.

Sweeten Up: If you'd like your drinks a little sweeter, don't add sugar. Use honey or Stevia instead. Stevia is a plant root that is ten times naturally sweeter than sugar. It is also high in fiber, so it's really a wonderful alternative to sugar. You can find it in health food stores or organically minded supermarkets like Whole Foods.

Pick A Winner

Be creative. You don't always have to combine veggies with veggies or fruits with fruits. Instead, try combining veggies and fruits together.

Adding a piece of fruit to an all veggie drink perks up the taste with that little bit of sweetness. Here's a list of the most ideal and healthful vegetables and fruits for juicing:

Apples, apricots, blueberries, broccoli, cabbage, carrots, cauliflower, celery, cucumber, fennel, grapes, kiwi, mango, melon, nectarines, oranges, peaches, pears, pineapple, plums, raspberries, tomatoes.

GINGER:

I have learned to acquire a taste for ginger because it has proven anti-cancer and anti-inflammatory properties. It also adds zip to any vegetable cocktail.

Because I use ginger in my daily veggie cocktail, I keep it in a ready-to-use form. I grate fresh, organically grown ginger, and then squeeze out the juice through a piece of cheesecloth. I store the extracted juice in a small container in the refrigerator. But, when adding ginger to your veggie cocktail, be stingy! It's quite potent, so you'll only need to add a few drops.

Va-Va-Va-Voom Veggie Cocktails

Here are some terrific veggie and fruit combos that produce delicious results. Just choose your favorite ingredients, then mix and match, going lighter on some and heavier on others. Remember, there are no rules. No matter how you combine them, the result is a vitamin and mineral winner!

Here are the ingredients for some other veggie cocktail combinations. You decide the proportions, according to your tastes. All of the veggies should be raw.

Red Hot Mamas

3 carrots

3 tomatoes

2 red bell peppers

1 teaspoon lemon juice

Jan's Daily Beta Carotene Boost

4 large carrots, washed and peeled

A few drops of organic ginger juice

Veggie Tips:

1. Always wash your vegetables and fruits thoroughly. There are many products available that remove any lingering pesticides or chemical residues on produce.

2. Pre-wash the veggies and store in plastic bags in the fridge for easy access.

3. Pre-peel carrots or any produce you use daily. So when you're in a hurry, your fruits and veggies are ready to go.

To Sum Up:

Make it as easy as possible on yourself so that you can juice every day. When the ingredients are already prepared and right at hand, you're much more likely to juice on a daily basis. With the ingredients ready to go, you can make a power-packed fruit or vegetable drink in under a minute!

Remember, these drinks are far superior to taking vitamins and minerals in pill form. Nature has already put them in the food, and in all the right proportions, too. All you need to do is juice a variety of these delicious whole foods every day for optimum health.

CHAPTER 12

Nutritious Foods: *The Good Earth*

MY FOOD PHILOSOPHY

Everything we need to stay healthy is growing here on earth. So, when you eat anything, always go for the most healthy and nutritious choice. Beliefs are the first step, but you must put them into practice—walk the walk, if you will.

Belief: Don't eat it unless it grows. Avoid processed and refined foods that are full of chemicals and have very little nutritional value.

Practice: When snacking, instead of eating sugary cookies from a package, eat an organically raised banana or apple.

—⁓—

Belief: All of the vitamins and minerals we need to support good health are found in fruits and vegetables. So it's important to eat a variety of them to meet your daily minimum requirements.

Practice: Steam two veggies with your dinner, one yellow (like corn or butternut squash) and one green. Instead of having a bowl of ice cream for dessert, make it a bowl of mixed berries.

———⟨⟨⟨⟩⟩⟩———

Belief: Avoid red meat that has been treated with hormones or other chemicals.
Practice: You can get your iron from green, leafy vegetables such as spinach, and your protein from beans or eggs.

———⟨⟨⟨⟩⟩⟩———

Belief: You can put only so much food into your body. Therefore, don't waste it on empty calories. Make smart choices about the most nourishing foods to eat.
Practice: Choose organic whole grain bread over processed white. Or choose to have double veggies with your dinner instead of one veggie and processed white rice.

———⟨⟨⟨⟩⟩⟩———

Belief: Carcinogens and other toxins in pesticides and fertilizers can get into ponds or other water supplies through runoff. They can eventually end up in our foods.
Practice: Don't eat certain farm-raised fish from waters that are polluted with pesticides and other run-off chemicals from the soil.

———⟨⟨⟨⟩⟩⟩———

Belief: Leave well enough alone. Eat foods as close to their natural state as possible, and don't cook all the vitamins and minerals out of them. Also, don't mess them up with cream sauces that provide nothing but calories and cholesterol in the form of bad fats.

Practice: Grill, broil, or bake your fish with lemon and low trans-fat margarine. Then season it with tasty, fresh herbs.

—◦◦◦—

Belief: Don't drink anything that fizzles or has cream in it. Sodas have no nutritional value, and creamy drinks are high in fats, calories, and bad cholesterols.

Practice: Learn to drink water, green tea, and fresh fruit and vegetable juices.

On The Lighter Side

Oh, I can just hear all of you cursing me out. I know you think that if you have to give up soft drinks, you'll lose the will to live. But honestly, all they do is add tons of calories, plus they make you bloated and gassy. Burp!

Belief: Because I had breast cancer, I try to choose foods that have proven anti-cancer properties.

Practice: Soy in various forms, like tofu and soybeans, contains *isoflavones*, which may inhibit estrogen-promoted breast cancers.

—◦◦◦—

Belief: Eat and drink in moderation. That way, you can avoid the risk of potentially overeating a food that may prove to be harmful at some future time.

Practice: There is still a lot of controversy about certain fish, like tuna, containing unsafe mercury levels. Get to know which fish are suspect, and eat them in moderation. You can always get plenty of protein from eating organic chicken, organic eggs, and vegetable dishes.

Belief: Avoid artificial sweeteners. They are made with unsafe chemicals and have no nutritional value. I have seen reports in magazines, newspapers and on television that claim aspartame can cause damage to the optic nerve and adversely affect certain neurotransmitters in the brain. **Practice:** Use only organic honey or Stevia, a plant root, to sweeten foods and drinks. Learn to acquire a taste for less sweet foods and a taste for beverages without any sweeteners in them.

KEEP IT SIMPLE: MY MENU REQUIREMENTS

1. It has to be made from whole foods.

2. It must be easy to prepare.

3. It should take thirty minutes or less to prepare.

Here is a sampling of my personal favorite menus for lunches and dinners.

Salads

I like to use organically grown spinach in my salads. I eat it about three times a week, as a lunch salad, a side dish with dinner, or as an entrée. Spinach not only has a good variety of vitamins, but it's also really high in iron. This is important for those of us who don't eat red meat.

Jan's Spinach and Strawberry Salad

1 bunch organically grown baby spinach

1 cup sliced organic strawberries

1 cup halved walnuts

1 cup cubed tofu

Dressing: Flaxseed oil and balsamic vinegar.

Variations: Add different nuts, substitute raspberries or blueberries, add feta cheese crumbles.

Spinach/Orange/Almond Salad

One bunch organic baby spinach leaves

1 cup slivered almonds

1 orange, peeled and sectioned

Dressing: 3 teaspoons extra-virgin olive oil or flaxseed oil

2 teaspoons low sodium soy sauce

4 teaspoons fresh lime juice

SALAD VERSATILITY

Salads are wonderful as side dishes but can also serve as an entire meal. Get creative. Here are just a few of the hundreds of variations you can make to turn a side salad into a nutritious entrée.

Vary your greens: It's a good idea to use different organically grown greens to make sure that you get all the vitamins and nutrients you can. Besides spinach, other healthy salad greens include romaine lettuce, bib lettuce, butter lettuce, endive, arugula, and various field greens.

Add protein: Protein may be added to salads in the form of chopped eggs, grilled shrimp, chicken, salmon, or a variety of beans, like garbanzos, and a variety of nuts.

Add fruits: I love to add blueberries or raspberries to spinach salads. Pears go well with endive or baby bib. If these fruits are out of season, you can thaw out frozen fruits or alternate with fruits that are always in season, like apples or grapes. Orange or grapefruit sections go well with shrimp or scallops and romaine.

Mushrooms: I often sauté delicious mushrooms, such as shiitakes, and add them to my spinach salads. Their flavor also goes well with the tofu cubes and flaxseed oil I mix into the salad.

Fish

I try to eat salmon twice a week because of the high omega 3 fatty acid content and other health benefits it provides. It's also a very versatile fish that can be prepared by grilling, baking, or poaching. This is one of my favorite ways to cook salmon, taught to me by my beloved Korean daughter-in-law, Whitney (Kyung) King:

Whitney's Salmon Marinade

Freshly squeezed juice of 3 organic oranges

1 cup low sodium soy sauce

Pinch of freshly grated ginger root

1 cup organic honey

Allow the fish to marinate for several hours. You may grill or bake the salmon. Whitney often adds a little honey on top of the fish because it bakes or grills into a yummy crust.

On The Lighter Side

I totally love my daughter-in-law, Whitney. Besides taking my son off my hands, she has produced three genetically perfect grandchildren for me and has managed to keep her weight the same as a croissant. Thanks to her teaching me about the basics of an Asian diet and following her recipes, I am a slim and healthy grandma (even though I'll never admit I'm old enough to be one!).

Jan's Baked Scallops

1 pound fresh sea scallops

1 cup panko bread crumbs

2 teaspoons organic lemon juice

¼ stick low trans-fat margarine

Place scallops in a Pyrex baking dish. Dot scallops with margarine, and squeeze lemon juice on them. Cover with a light layer of panko bread crumbs. Bake in a 350° oven for 30 minutes.

Whitney's Stir-Fry Shrimp or Scallops

1 cup broccoli florets

1 cup cauliflower florets

1 cup Chinese peas

1 cup zucchini cubes

1 cup bok choy

1 cup sesame or extra virgin olive oil

¼ cup oyster sauce

Stir fry the veggies in sesame oil or olive oil. Add a little oyster sauce and cornstarch to thicken. Toss in the shrimp or scallops, and stir fry for a few more minutes until done. Add your favorite seasonings, such as toasted sesame seeds or paprika, as you stir fry.

Tomatoes: The Super Food

You can do just about anything with tomatoes. They can be added uncooked into salads, cooked and served in pasta dishes, or stewed with other veggies. The beauty of tomatoes is that cooking will not destroy the nutritious lycopene in them.

Herb-Broiled Tomatoes

Sprinkle breadcrumbs, basil, and shredded Parmesan cheese on halved tomatoes. Run them under the broiler for about five minutes.

Fresh Tomato Salad

Alternate slices of fresh, organic tomatoes with buffalo mozzarella cheese. Drizzle with flaxseed or extra-virgin olive oil vinaigrette and sprinkle with fresh basil or oregano.

Soups

I love to make soups all year round. The beauty of soup is that it can be stocked with a whole variety of nutritious vegetables, beans, and whole grains, such as barley.

I prefer tomato or vegetable broth-based soups. But certain creamy soups, like pea, acorn squash or broccoli, also pack a nutritious punch. You don't always have to pass on these, because they can be made with very light cream or even a yogurt base. Some of my favorite soups are vegetable, minestrone, split pea, acorn, and butternut squash.

Desserts

We all love them, but I try to pass on them as much as possible. Most of those yummy, sinful desserts are filled with butter, starch, and sugar! If I am still hungry after dinner, I try to eat whole food desserts, like berries sweetened with organic honey. An occasional low-sugar, fresh fruit sorbet is also a smart choice. If I am craving ice cream, I'll indulge myself with one of those mini-ice cream sandwich bars made with soy. They contain no milk or creams and are only sixty calories.

Baked Apples

This dish satisfies a sweet tooth and nutritional needs. You may use your favorite organically grown apples, like Fuji, Gala, Delicious, or Granny Smith.

6 apples, cored

Fill with a mixture of honey, cinnamon, nutmeg, and chopped walnuts. Bake at 350° for 30 minutes. Baste apples a few times while cooking

Snacks

Snacking is pretty much everyone's downfall. It would be ideal if we could get through a whole day without snacking in between meals. But, unfortunately, most of us don't have an iron will. So the next best thing is to make smart snack choices. Make a rule for yourself to only snack on whole foods. Here are some smart choices:

• Raisin and nut mix

- Nonfat yogurt
- Ice-cold grapes
- Nuts
- Unbuttered, unsalted popcorn
- Frozen banana
- Carrots and celery sticks
- An apple, peach, pear, or orange
- Sorbets made with fresh fruit and no sugars

On The Lighter Side

Lots of people swear they only have one drink a day. But they forget to tell you that it's in a one gallon glass!

Alcohol

Oh, I just know you want to hear what I have to say about this topic! I can understand how people who follow the healthy path of avoiding sugars, fats, and red meats lose the will to live if they can't have a glass of wine or alcoholic beverage once in a while.

Sure, it's okay to have a glass of wine or two. But, everything in moderation is the key here. I hardly ever drink alcohol. If I do, it's a glass of champagne. I don't drink for the following reasons:

1. I don't like the taste.
2. I don't want to waste the calories on booze.
3. It makes me so sleepy that it interferes with my exercise regimen.

Also, it has been my observation over the years that drinkers age faster than nondrinkers. I think it dries you up from the inside out. Often I can tell drinkers just from looking at their skin. Their faces and bodies are a bit flaccid, they have more wrinkles, and their skin doesn't have the moist, healthy glow that nondrinkers have.

On The Lighter Side

Hey, I don't mean to get up on my prohibition soapbox here. But, I am telling you the truth. My personal motto is: Drink like a fish, look like a prune.

However, that's just my opinion. I am aware of the research that shows grapes are a naturally rich source of antioxidants. So a glass of wine at dinner can be a good thing. The trick is to drink in moderation. Go ahead and God bless. Relax and enjoy your life!

DIETING

I do not believe in diets for losing weight. From my experience with nutrition, it's *what* you put into your body that makes the difference. You can choose an 800-calorie bowl of ice cream, full of fats and sugar, or a 60-calorie soy bar. You can start with a basic 500-calorie fish and vegetable dinner, add a saturated fat cream sauce and mashed potatoes, and transform it into an unhealthy 1,200-calorie meal.

Eating healthy foods is not just about weight but it also makes all the difference in your health. I've seen it firsthand. My husband was overweight, had borderline diabetes and fat in his liver. After following a healthy nutritional plan recommended to him by a nutritionist, my husband lost 32 pounds, his blood sugar dropped to normal, and all the fat in his liver disappeared! Nobody can argue with these results.

What you eat will not only determine your weight, but ultimately your state of health. The wrong diet can do harmful things to the body. It can:

• Raise your blood pressure
• Clog your arteries
• Make you obese
• Put fat in your organs
• Help the onset of diabetes
• Cause malnutrition
• Zap your energy
• Cause any number of skin problems

- Damage your vision
- Ultimately kill you

Don't waste your time and your good health eating non-nutritious foods. Think of food as medicine that supports all body functions and prevents disease. When you really start believing this, you will be ready to make the dietary changes to start eating healthy as a way of life.

CHAPTER 13

Exercise:
The Gift That Keeps On Giving

MOVE IT, MOVE IT, MOVE IT

To enjoy good health, have plenty of energy, and be fit enough to handle anything life throws at you, you need only two things:

1. A nourishing, whole food diet
2. A regular exercise regimen

These are the keys to having it all.

Nourishing foods are a must to build and repair the body's cells, tissues, and immune system. Our circulatory systems have been designed to deliver molecular oxygen and nutrients to every cell in our bodies and remove toxins the same way. This system works most efficiently when blood is being forcefully pumped around our bodies during exercise.

Think about it. The heart and arteries have muscular walls designed to pump the blood and keep it moving. Inactivity makes muscle weak and flaccid. If the circulatory system isn't working efficiently, our organs won't get their maximum nutrients and toxin removal is slower. The result is health problems.

It's too bad we can't actually peer inside our bodies and see how exercise helps every one of our organs function better. However, there is one organ we can see, and it tells us a lot about our general state of health. That organ is our skin.

OUR SKIN: A BAROMETER OF HEALTH

The skin is actually the largest organ in the body. Besides being the protective covering of the body, it has other functions as well. It contains nerve endings for sensory and temperature sensation. It contains pores and sweat glands that rid the body of toxins. It also has a rich supply of tiny blood vessels that keep the skin alive by delivering nutrients and oxygen and removing systemic wastes.

I think a person's skin tells a lot about her general state of health. For example, I can pretty much tell if a person smokes just from the appearance of his skin. A smoker's skin looks dried out, it's more wrinkled and has less tone and often an unhealthy pallor. Why is this? Because nicotine and other toxins found in cigarettes constrict blood vessels and, thus, inhibit the distribution of oxygen and nutrients and the removal of wastes.

By comparison, look at the skin of a person who has just finished exercising. It's moist, has a rosy color, and seems to glow. This is because exercise has forced more blood to the surface, and you can actually see the results of that organ working optimally.

Try to picture all of your other organs looking and working their best, as the result of regular exercise. Trust me, I've been doing it for more than thirty years. Exercise will dramatically improve the quality of your life.

No More Excuses

Here are the five cardinal rules of exercise I live by.

The Rules Of Exercise

1. DO it regularly
2. You must SWEAT
3. VARY your routines
4. PUSH yourself by setting new goals
5. For MOTIVATION, choose a role model

On The Lighter Side

A heavy-set friend of mine jokes that she's been working out to get into shape—Round is a shape!

Exercise Regularly: In my opinion, it doesn't matter so much *what* kind of exercise you do, as long as you *do it on a regular basis*. What is regularly? I think every other day is a minimum. But remember, the more frequently you work out, the more you benefit. This is an area in your life where it is *not* in your best interest to just try and *get by*. You are exercising to help your body maintain good health. So, why would you want to cheat yourself? The harder you work out, and the more you work out, the bigger the health benefit for you.

The secret is to pick an exercise you really like and go with it. If you don't know what you like, try taking some classes at your gym, such as spinning, kickboxing, or aerobics, and see what you take a shine to. Or just start running or power walking around your neighborhood. Whatever you do, the important thing is to like it enough to do it on a regular basis.

Do Sweat It: I have to laugh when I hear women saying that they like such-and-such a class because they don't sweat in it. Not sweat? Excuse me. Aren't you defeating the whole purpose of working out?

Sweating is necessary. It means you're working your heart muscle and your blood is pumping oxygen and removing toxins all around the body. Push yourself. Exercise is *supposed* to be hard work! So for your own health and well-being, you must make that commitment to incorporate a regular exercise regimen in your life.

On The Lighter Side

Listen to me, girls. For heaven's sake, don't be one of those creampuff women who goes to the gym with her hair done, in full makeup and a designer aerobics outfit— and then is afraid to sweat. You're wasting your time. Going to the gym like this isn't going to gain you anything except a few extra pounds—and possibly, a guy.

Vary Your Routines: Often, when we find a particular exercise regimen we like, we just stick to that one, without variation. Granted, we all like our comfort zones. But, in my opinion, you're shortchanging yourself. The body has many different muscles that all need to be exercised. Repeating the same exercises, day after day, won't get to all of your muscle groups. Some regimens are more aerobic, some are more cardio, and others, like weight lifting, are nonaerobic. Each one has its own particular area of the body that benefits.

That's why doing a variety of exercises is best for the body. Many classes devote an extra fifteen to thirty minutes for weight lifting or floor exercises. For example, if you do a fifty minute step aerobic class, your heart muscle and leg muscles are getting the majority of the workout. But it isn't targeting the muscles in your upper body. So by adding a few extra minutes of light weight lifting and some resistance training, such as resistance bands or ball, you'll get a *total body workout.*

Exercise Options

Aerobics (high and low impact)	Yoga
Cycling (also called spinning)	Resist-a-ball (Swiss ball)
Cardio-kickboxing	Core training
Power boxing	Weight lifting
Step aerobics	Boot camp (a little of everything)
Step interval with weights	Running
Pilates	Walking

Exercise Machines

Treadmill

Stepper

Elliptical

Stationary bicycle

Rowing

Plus at least a dozen different varieties of other machines that exercise specific muscles in the body, like the abs or legs, etc.

On The Lighter Side

Hold the phone! I forgot to mention the mini-trampoline. This fabbo little gizmo will not only get your blood pumping and your endorphins flowing, it's also easy on the joints. So get one and bounce your way to bliss, baybee!

I prefer taking classes in the gym because they keep up with the latest exercise trends, based on research in their field. Also, working out with my friends in the classes helps keep me motivated. But no matter what venue you choose, the idea is to vary your regimens to get the overall body benefits.

The Home Gym: Because of work or other time constraints, many people are able to workout regularly only if they have one or more pieces of equipment, such as a treadmill, in their homes. That's an excellent idea. Anything that will facilitate your being able to work out regularly is a wise investment. You can buy a good treadmill for practically the same price as a year's membership to a gym.

Exercising doesn't have to be expensive. The only cost is your time and dedication. You can purchase a step and risers cheaply and do your step aerobics at home. Or, you don't even need any equipment. Just buy an aerobics or kickboxing tape and get busy. Cheaper still, you can power walk or run around your neighborhood for free.

There is just no excuse for not finding the thirty/sixty minutes every day or every other day to do something beneficial for yourself.

Keep Setting New Goals: We all get complacent. Therefore, it's important to become aware of the need to keep challenging yourself. When you start feeling like your exercise routine is becoming pretty easy, it's time to kick it up a notch. You might accomplish this by adding more weight to your lifting regimen, running more miles, or stepping up the pace from low to high impact aerobics. But no matter how you do it, you'll get the best results for your body when you keep pushing yourself.

Set new goals for yourself periodically. You might want to lose five pounds in a month, or tone up your abs enough to fit into size-eight slacks. Whatever. It's all doable. You might start by running three miles on the treadmill, instead of two. However, to keep up your workouts on a regular basis, you must stay motivated. And the way you stay motivated is by periodically setting new goals for yourself.

Role Models: I know how tough it can be to stay motivated enough to work out every day. So, I'll let you in on my little secret. From the time I was a kid, I always had role models I emulated. And, as an adult, I still have them!

My hero and role model is Lance Armstrong. He not only beat a stage four cancer that his doctors said had realistically only about a three percent survival rate, but he also recovered and went on to compete in the most physical and mental contest ever invented, the Tour de France. And he won it seven times! The man's incredible. I keep a poster of him next to my computer, and when I'm feeling blocked and tired, I look at him and say to myself: "Get your butt in gear, and keep pushing. Look at Lance. He *never* gave up."

On The Lighter Side

And, if the noble image of Lance doesn't work, I take a good, hard look in the mirror at my poochy belly and midriff bulge. That kind of reality is the ultimate motivation!

When I'm in the gym, flaking out on some of the more exhausting moves, I picture Lance in a fetal position, when his body was ravaged by chemo. Then I picture him building up his strength by getting back on his bicycle. Then I see him sailing through the finish tape at the Tour de France! And you know what? It makes me push myself even harder. Like Lance, I thank God I am alive and healthy enough to be able to be working out.

To Sum Up:

There is absolutely no doubt that since having cancer, these past seven years have been the best of my life, so far. The changes I made in my diet and my commitment to exercise have given me brimming good health, confidence, and spiritual strength. But they just didn't come out of nowhere. I had to make changes in my life, work harder, and make certain sacrifices in order to achieve it. But my efforts have been *more* than worth it. The payoff has been huge.

When you eat nourishing whole foods, exercise regularly, and practice the Bounce plan, you can expect to have the following things in your life, on a daily basis:

- You'll wake up feeling good, with a sense of well-being.
- You'll have fewer colds, flus, and other ailments.
- Your weight will become more manageable.
- Your body will be more toned and youthful.
- Your normal state of mind will be happy.
- You'll have peace in your life.
- You'll look younger.
- You won't live in fear of adversity because you have the tools to overcome it.
- Your energies will be spent in positive and creative directions.
- You'll live in the *now*, with an attitude of gratitude.

RECAP: THE BOUNCE PLAN

Let's do it one more time! I want to make sure that by now you have integrated the steps of the Bounce plan into your thinking. For any problem that besets you, working toward a resolution will require enormous energy, stamina, and focus. Following the six principles of the Bounce plan will be of invaluable help to you. It will keep you strong enough to act with patience and wisdom. Let's take them one by one:

BE POSITIVE:

Before the skies clear, there will be lots of rainy days ahead. Therefore, you'll need to remain positive and optimistic. There will be a light at the end of the tunnel—for everyone concerned. Trust me. Once you face the issues and begin working on resolutions, everyone in your life will eventually get to a better place. However, it takes time and perseverance. So always remember to face each day seeing that glass half-full.

OVERCOME STRESS:

Now is the time to begin meditating for the rest of your life. When your emotions start swinging like a yo-yo, it's imperative to gain control over them by centering yourself. And the most direct way of accomplishing serenity is through daily meditation. It is the most powerful and effective tool you can use. In fact, it's more effective than any tranquilizer on the market.

I know that many people think of meditation as a kind of weird, occult practice. But, honestly, it's one of the most natural things you can do—just like breathing. Meditation is really just sitting quietly in a chair for twenty minutes, trying to clear your mind of stray thoughts. It's a little bit hard at first because the mind tends to "chatter" from inner turmoil. So to help clear the chatter, you simply focus on your breathing or repeat a word (mantra), such as "ohm."

If you're really intimidated, I recommend listening to Dr. Wayne Dyer's tapes on meditating, or try reading Jon Kabat Zinn's *Wherever You Go, There You Are*. You'll find that with practice it gets easier, and if practiced every day, it's the most effective way of calming and focusing yourself.

UPLIFT YOURSELF:

Surround yourself with people (single and married), who live happy, well-adjusted lives. Stay away from bars or places where unhappy people drown their problems with alcohol. Remember, misery loves company. You need to be with clear-headed people who can offer positive and wise advice that is not based on anger and revenge.

Avoid watching depressing movies or spending time listening to melancholy music. Don't waste valuable time wallowing in self-pity and misery. Your goal is to rise above it and bounce back to happiness.

NATURAL FOODS:

When your life gets tumultuous, you probably won't feel like cooking for yourself, and you'll be more tempted to fill up on junk foods. Normally, during periods of stress, people overeat or stop eating altogether. Be careful not to fall into either trap. Instead, start nourishing your body with the most wholesome, organically grown foods as possible.

When we are upset or feeling guilty, we often seek solace in comfort foods. Avoid sugars and caffeine, because these chemicals will exacerbate anxiety and depression. Your immune system is being depressed by stress, and in turn, every organ in your body could pay the price. The key to remaining strong and focused is *energy*. So pay special attention to fueling your body with only the most nourishing and pure foods available.

COUNSELING:

When problems become overwhelming, don't be adverse to getting help. Don't make the excuse that you can't afford it. You can't afford *not* to. Counseling will help you begin thinking more analytically and less emotionally. Therefore, you'll make better decisions. Talking over problems with a skilled therapist will give you a clearer perspective, which helps decrease your stress level. A good counselor will navigate you through your conflicts and help you to make the choices that will lead to lasting resolutions.

EXERCISE:

Regular exercise is critical for releasing the endorphins your body desperately needs to lift depression, lessen anxiety, and provide the energy you need to handle constant stress. You can exercise in the gym, run, walk, play tennis, or any other way. Any kind of exercise will provide lasting benefits, *as long as* it's done on a regular basis. When going through a crisis, I strongly recommend that you exercise every day. The harmful effects of continual stress and pressure need to be counteracted with immune-strengthening exercise.

So there you have it. The Bounce plan is a way of life. It is not based on anything unrealistic or mystical. It's simply a way of living your life on a positive track, by focusing on your own wellness. And, when you do this, it empowers you. The principles in the Bounce plan come from loving yourself enough to take the best care of yourself as possible. And, when you do this, everyone else in your life will benefit from your example and your results.

So, remember: B-O-U-N-C-E. Internalize it. Practice it. Live it. Then, rebound into life, happier and healthier than ever!

References

Brownstein, Art, M.D., M.P.H. *Extraordinary Healing*. Gig Harbor, Washington: Harbor Press, 2005.

Francis, Raymond, M.Sc., and Cotton, Kester. *Never Be Sick Again*. Deerfield Beach, FL: Health Communications, Inc., 2002.

Siple, Molly, M.S., R.D. *Healing For Dummies*. New York: IDG Books Worldwide, Inc., 1999.

Schwarcz, Joe, Ph.D., and Berkoff, Fran, R.D. *Foods That Harm and Foods That Heal*. New York: Reader's Digest Association, Inc., 2004.

Weil, Andrew, M.D. *Spontaneous Healing*. New York: Ballantine Books, 1995.